THE BEST OF TOFU

This beautifully illustrated book presents tofu at its best. Besides traditional tofu cooking, which retains authentic flavors, it contains a variety of easy-to-follow inventive recipes. Included are twenty-five irresistible varieties of chilled tofu, twenty-four dishes in which tofu plays a leading role, fourteen simple menus that go well with drinks, twelve hot pot dishes, four dishes made with preserved tofu, eight tofu desserts, and four fascinating recipes using okara , the by-product that remains when soy milk is pressed out of soybeans. Techniques of making tofu at home are illustrated step-by-step. The draining techniques, methods of preservation, and cutting methods are also illustrated, and anyone who is unfamiliar with tofu can easily follow them. The explanations about all the varieties of tofu and their nutritional value will be useful background material when you try some of these recipes.

JUNKO TAKAGI

CONTENTS

■Notes

The two most popular types of tofu in Japan are momen (cotton) tofu and kinugoshi (silken) tofu. The former is often called regular tofu. Chinese-style tofu, which has a meaty texture, is generally called 'firm tofu.' Japanese-style tofu is prized for its softer and more delicate texture. The principal ingredient of each recipe is one cake (about 300 g / 10.5 oz) of tofu.

●1 Tbsp (tablespoon) = 15 cc, 1 tsp (teaspoon) = 5 cc, 1 cup = 200 cc. (In Japan, one cup equals 200 cc; in the United States, 240 cc)

●Unless noted, use dark soy sauce, rice vinegar, natural salt, and cake flour.

●Dashi or basic stock is made from kombu and dried bonito flakes. You may also use commercially available powdered soup stock.

●Chicken stock is made from boiled chicken parts. You may also use commercially available powdered chicken soup.

●These recipes assume that you are using a 500 W microwave oven. Multiple the times by 1.2 if you are using a 400 W oven, and by 0.8 if you are using a 600 W oven. Since electrical power varies, make sure that you know the correct wattage of your oven.

REGULAR TOFU COOKING

Translated by Kazuhiko Nagai and Karen Sandness

© 2004 English tex., Japan Publications Trading Co., Ltd.
English edition by Japan Publications Trading Co., Ltd., 1-2-1 Sarugaku-cho, Chiyoda-ku, Tokyo 101-0064, Japan.
First edition: First printing : October 2004

Original Japanese edition by Nihon Bungei-sha Co., Ltd., 1-7 Kanda Jinbo-cho, Chiyoda-ku, Tokyo 101-8407, Japan.

Distributors:
United States: Kodansha America, Inc. through Oxford University Press, 198 Madison Avenue, New York, NY 10016.
Canada: Fitzhenry and Whiteside, 195 Allestate Parkway, Ontario L3R 4T8.
Australia and New Zealand: Bookwise International Pty Ltd. 174 Cormack Road, Wingfield, South Australia, Australia.
Asia and Japan: Japan Publications Trading Co., Ltd., 1-2-1 Sarugaku-co, Chiyoda-ku, Tokyo 101-0064, Japan.

ISBN: 4-88996-172-0
Printed in Japan

REGULAR TOFU COOKING

Presented here are some traditional Japanese tofu dishes.
These four recipes are familiar to everyone.
The first time you make these recipes, follow them exactly.
Subsequently you can vary them according to your own preferences.

⦿ SIMMERED TOFU
(Yu-dofu)

Use the choicest ingredients to make this simple but satisfying dish. Eat it with homemade tosa-joyu (dipping sauce) and your favorite condiments.

O Ingredients
1 cake momen tofu
10-15 cm (4-6 in) kombu
Broth
⅓ cup soy sauce
3 Tbsp water
3 Tbsp dried bonito flakes

O Method
❶ Cut the tofu into 8 cubes.
❷ Wipe the kombu with a wet cloth and spread it on the bottom of a pot. Pour the dipping sauce into a container and place it in the middle of the pot. Add the tofu and water to the pot and place it over heat.
● Tosa-joyu
Heat the broth ingredients in a pot. When it comes to a boil, turn off the heat.
※ You may strain the bonito flakes or leave them whole as you wish.

Garnishes

Sudachi (citrus fruit), cayenne pepper, mixture of cayenne pepper and six other spices, fresh ginger, scallion, citron peel.

CHILLED TOFU

(Hiya-yakko)

Be sure to soak the tofu in clear water beforehand.

○ **Ingredients**

1 cake momen tofu
1 piece of fresh ginger
a 10 cm (4 in) scallion
Soy sauce to taste

○ **Method**

❶ Press the excess liquid from the tofu by hand. Briefly soak it in water in a bowl and then transfer it to a bamboo colander to drain. Cut it into four to six cubes.

❷ Grate the ginger and cut the scallion into round slices from the end.

❸ Transfer the tofu to a container and top with condiments. Pour soy sauce over, if desired.

Garnishes

Grated wasabi / scallion cut
into round slices

Grated ginger / Chives cut
into round slices

Toasted sesame seeds /
Julienne green perilla

Buds of red perillas /
Julienne Japanese
ginger soaked in water
and drained

MA PO TOFU

Enjoy the sharp and spicy taste.

Doubanjiang
(Hot Bean Sauce)

A Chinese paste of seasoned and fermented soybeans, broad beans and chopped red chili pepper. It is mainly used for Sichuan cuisine.

Tianmianjiang
(Sweet Bean Sauce)

A Chinese paste made of soybeans, flour and salt by a process of repeated heating and fermentation. It is used for Peking Duck and Twice-Cooked Pork.

Ingredients

1 cake momen tofu
100 g (3½ oz) ground pork (lean)
⅓ scallion, chopped
1 small clove garlic, chopped
1 piece of fresh ginger, chopped
½ Tbsp doubanjiang (hot bean paste)

Sauce

1 Tbsp tianmianjiang
1½ Tbsp soy sauce
½ tsp sugar
2 Tbsp sake
¾ cup chicken stock
2 Tbsp salad oil
3 Tbsp dissolved cornstarch (1 part water and 2 parts cornstarch)
Some ground Sichuan pepper
5 cm (2 in) scallion

Method

❶Drain the tofu in a bamboo colander and dice into 1.5 cm (½ in) cubes.

❷Combine the sauce ingredients and mix well.

❸Preheat a wok well and coat the inside with the salad oil. Add and stir-fry the ground pork over high neat.

❹When the meat is well browned, add the garlic, ginger, green onion and hot bean paste in this order. When this mixture is well flavored, add w and stir-fry thoroughly. Add the chicken stock.

❺When the mixture comes to a boil, add the tofu and mix well. When it comes to a boil again, swirl the dissolved cornstarch into it.

❻Transfer the mixture to a platter, sprinkle with Sichuan pepper, and scatter chopped green onion over it.

DEEP-FRIED TOFU WITH AMBER SAUCE

(Agedashi-tofu)

This is one of the most popular tofu dishes.

Ingredients

1 cake tofu
Grated daikon radish
Grated fresh ginger
Scallions, cut into thin round slices
$\frac{1}{6}$ cup flour
$\frac{1}{6}$ cup cornstarch
Oil for deep-frying

Amber sauce
$\frac{1}{2}$ cup dashi stock
1 Tbsp mirin (sweet rice wine)
$\frac{1}{2}$ Tbsp soy sauce
$\frac{1}{5}$ tsp salt

Method

❶Wrap the tofu in a dry cloth. Press lightly on top to remove excess water. Cut it in half.
❷Mix the flour and cornstarch. Coat the tofu with the mixture. Let it stand for 5 minutes, and then coat it again.
❸Deep-fry in oil preheated to 180℃ (360F°) until golden brown.
❹Combine the amber sauce ingredients and bring them to a boil. When the sauce has boiled, turn off the heat.
❺Transfer the hot tofu to a small bowl. Top with grated radish, grated ginger and green onions. Fill the bowl with the hot amber sauce.

TOFU COATED WITH SESAME SEEDS

(Goma-dare)
A variation of agedashi-tofu. The Chinese-style sauce is a bit spicy.

Ingredients

1 block momen tofu
3 Tbsp flour
2 Tbsp water
$\frac{1}{2}$ egg
4-5 Tbsp each of white and black sesame seeds
Oil for deep-frying

Coating
2 Tbsp vinegar
2 Tbsp sugar
3 Tbsp soy sauce
1 tsp doubanjiang
$\frac{1}{2}$ tsp sesame oil

Method

❶Drain the tofu and cut it into 6 cubes. (See p.99)
❷Mix the water and egg in a bowl. Add the flour and mix well.
❸Soak the tofu pieces in the coating mixture and cover them with sesame seeds.
❹Deep-fry the tofu in oil preheated to 175℃ (350F°) until crispy.
❺Transfer the tofu to a bowl and pour the remaining sauce over it.

HIYA-YAKKO AND SALAD-YAKKO

(Chilled Tofu Topped with Salad)

Presented here are a variety of tofu dishes, some simple and others fancy.
You can enjoy them all the year round.

Simple Japanese-style chilled tofu

⦿FRIED YOUNG SARDINES

Green perillas taste better when cut into strips and soaked in cold water.

O Ingredients
1 cake momen tofu
15 g (½ oz) dried young sardines
2 Tbsp salad oil
4 green perillas
Sesame seeds
Soy sauce

O Method
❶Heat the salad oil in a frying pan. Add the young sardines and stir-fry them until crispy. Transfer them to a paper towel.
❷Cut the green perilla into thin strips. Dip it in cold water briefly and drain. Toast the sesame seeds.
❸Put the sardines and perilla on top of the tofu. Drip soy sauce on it if you desire.

⦂NATTO
(Fermented Soybeans)
This goes well with boiled rice.

O Ingredients
1 pack yose tofu (see p. 68)
40 g (1⅖ oz) natto
2 tsp soy sauce
1 stalk of chives, chopped into thin slices

O Method
❶Chop the natto chunks into smaller pieces.
Add soy sauce and chives. Mix well.
❷Ladle the tofu into a bowl and top it with
the mixture.
※You may use cracked natto instead of
regular natto.

⦂KAYAKU
(Assortment of Pickled Vegetables)
Use your favorite pickled vegetables.

O Ingredients
1 pack yose tofu (see p. 68)
15 g (½ oz) takuan (pickled daikon radish)
20 g (⅔ oz) shibazuke (assorted vegetables
pickled with perilla)
20 g (⅔ oz) pickled cucumber

O Method
❶Chop up the takuan, shibazuke, and
cucumber separately.
❷Ladle the tofu into a bowl and arrange the
three kinds of chopped pickles on top.

Chilled Tofu Topped with Hot Sauce

SHIITAKE MUSHROOMS AND BAMBOO SHOOTS

Use your favorite mushrooms to make this sauce.

O Ingredients

1 cake momen tofu
2 dried shiitake mushrooms
50 g (1¾ oz) boiled bamboo shoots
½ – ⅔ cup chicken stock

Broth

½ Tbsp each of sake and soy sauce
½ tsp sugar
1 tsp sesame oil

O Method

❶Soak the shiitakes in water until tender. Trim away the hard top and cut the mushrooms into thin slices. Cut bamboo shoots into 2 cm (¾ in) lengths.
❷Pour the chicken stock into a pot. Add the mushrooms, bamboo shoots, and broth, and cook until the shiitakes are well seasoned.
❸Cut the tofu into cubes and transfer it to a plate. Pour the heated mixture over it.

⚙HOT SESAME OIL

Hot sesame oil brings out a savory aroma.

○ SCALLIONS WITH SALT
(Green Onions and Salt)

○ Ingredients
1 cake momen tofu
¼ scallion
⅕ tsp salt
Powdered pepper
1 Tbsp sesame oil

○ Method
❶Cut the tofu in half. Chop up the scallion.
❷Sprinkle salt over the tofu. Top with the scallion and sprinkle with powdered pepper.
❸Heat the sesame oil in a small pan. When it starts smoking, pour it over the tofu.

○ GREEN ONIONS AND ZASAI

○ Ingredients
1 cake momen tofu
3 green onions
30 g (1 oz) zasai (pickled mustard tuber)
(See p. 86)
1 Tbsp dried bonito flakes
2 tsp or 1 Tbsp soy sauce
1 Tbsp sesame oil

○ Method
❶Cut the tofu in half. Rinse the zasai in water and cut it into thin slices. Rinse again while rubbing and then chop it in large pieces. Cut the green onions into thin round slices starting at the tip.
❷Put the zasai, green onions and bonito flakes on the tofu.
❸Heat the sesame oil in a small pan. When the oil starts smoking, put it over the tofu.

MIXTURE OF MEAT AND MISO

This hearty sauce is good to have on hand.

Ingredients

1 cake silken tofu
40 g (1½ oz) ground pork
¼ tsp garlic, chopped
¼ tsp minced fresh ginger

Sauce

1 Tbsp red miso
3 Tbsp water
1 tsp sake
½ tsp mirin
⅓ tsp each of sugar and soy sauce
¾ tsp sesame oil
Dash of pepper

Salad oil

Method

❶Heat the salad oil in a frying pan and sauté the garlic and ginger. Add the ground pork and stir-fry over high heat.

❷When the meat is browned add the sauce ingredients and continue stir-frying until the mixture is slightly scorched and you can smell a delicious aroma.

❸Lay the tofu in a container and top it with the meat and miso mixture.

FRAGRANT STIR FRY

Put assortments of stir-fried ingredients on top of tofu.

Ingredients
1 cake silken tofu
40 g (1½ oz) leek
½ Tbsp dried shrimp
5 cm (2 in) scallion
½ piece of fresh ginger
⅛ tsp salt
Dash of pepper
½ Tbsp sake
1 tsp sesame oil

Method
❶Chop up the scallion and ginger. Cut the leek into 6 mm (¼ in) lengths. Soak the dried shrimp in lukewarm water until tender and chop it.
❷Heat the sesame oil in a frying pan and stir-fry the shrimp. When you can smell the shrimp, add the scallion and leek and stir-fry. Season with salt, pepper and sake.
❸Put the stir-fried mixture on top of the tofu.

STIR-FRIED NOZAWANA AND GREEN PEPPER

You may use leaf mustard instead of nozawana. This chilled tofu dish goes well with boiled rice.

Ingredients
1 cake silken tofu
1 green pepper
30 g (1 oz) nozawana
A bit of fresh ginger
1 cm (⅜ in) scallion
Sauce
  ⅓ tsp sugar
  1 tsp sake
  ⅔ tsp soy sauce
  Dash of salt
½ Tbsp salad oil

Method
❶Cut off the ends of the green pepper and remove the seeds. Cut into 2 cm (¾ in) strips. Chop the nozawana and stir-fry it in a dry pan until the moisture boils off.
❷Chop the ginger and scallion.
❸Heat the salad oil in a frying pan and stir-fry the ginger and scallion. When you can smell the ginger and scallion, add the nozawana and stir-fry. Season with the soy sauce mixture.
❹Put the stir-fried ingredients on top of the tofu.

CHINESE-STYLE YAKKO

⚙SHOYU SAUCE

A popular Chinese hors d'oeuvre with a colorful ginger-flavored topping.

Ingredients
1 cake silken tofu
1 pidan (preserved duck egg)
2 Tbsp dried shrimp
2 cherry tomatoes

Sauce
¾ Tbsp vinegar
1⅓ Tbsp soy sauce
½ tsp sesame oil
Dash of chili oil
⅔ tsp ginger juice
1-2 stems of fresh coriander

Method
❶Shell the pidan and cut into 6 to 8 pieces vertically. Stir-fry the dried shrimp briefly in a bit of salad oil (extra) and chop it coarse pieces. Trim away the ends of the cherry tomatoes and cut them into 8 parts.
❷Combine the sauce ingredients.
❸Cut the tofu into 8 cubes and place it on a plate. Top it with ingredients ❶ and pour the sauce over it. Sprinkle shredded coriander over it.

⬭PIDAN
A preserved duck egg. The raw egg is smeared with a mixture of salt, lime, tea, and ashes, coated with chaff, put into an urn with a lid, and matured for 15 to 30 days. The egg white turns brown and jellifies. The egg yolk turns greenish brown and becomes soft.

SESAME PASTE SAUCE

A variation of the popular cold chicken dish flavored with a sesame dressing, substantial enough to be a main dish.

O Ingredients

1 cake momen tofu
1 eggplant
70 g (2½ oz) chicken breast
Dash of salt and pepper
Dash of sake
10 cm (4 in) scallion (green part)
1 piece of fresh ginger, sliced thinly
1 small tomato
(A) ½ Tbsp zhimajiang
    1 Tbsp ground toasted sesame seeds
    2 tsp vinegar
    ⅓ tsp sugar
    1 Tbsp soy sauce
    ⅓ tsp sesame oil
    Dash of chili oil
(B) ½ tsp minced scallion
    ½ tsp minced fresh ginger
    ⅓ French mustard

O Method

❶Trim and peel the eggplant. Place it on a microwave-safe dish and cover it with plastic wrap. Heat it in a microwave oven for 1 minute or 1minute 20 seconds. Cut it in half and then slice it diagonally into 1 cm (⅜ in) widths.

❷Place the chicken meat in a microwave-safe dish. Season it with salt and pepper. Sprinkle it with a dash of sake. Add the scallion and ginger and cover with plastic wrap. Heat it in a microwave oven for 1 minute 30 seconds or 2 minutes. Wait until the meat is cold and then shred it by hand. Cut the tomato into thin slices.

❸Put the zhimajiang, vinegar, and sugar into a bowl in this order and mix well. Add the other ingredients from (A) and mix until smooth. Mix in the ingredients from (B).

❹Cut the tofu in half and place it on a plate. Garnish with the eggplant and the chicken mixture and top with the sesame paste sauce.

ZHIMAJIANG (Sesame Seed Paste)

A creamy paste of ground toasted white sesame seeds and vegetable oil. It has a rich, nutty flavor and is used as a sauce for cold chicken meat dish.

KOCHUJAN SAUCE

The unique taste of kochujan goes well with seafood.

O Ingredients

1 cake momen tofu
50 g (1¾ oz) boiled octopus
20 g (⅔ oz) wakame seaweed
10 cm (4 in) scallion

Sauce

1 Tbsp kochujan (chili paste)
½ Tbsp miso
½ Tbsp sugar
2 Tbsp soy sauce
1 tsp sesame oil
½ tsp grated garlic
4 Tbsp water

O Method

❶Rinse the octopus, wipe away the water, and then cut it into 1 cm (⅜ in) pieces. Cut the wakame seaweed into 2 cm (¾ in) lengths. Cut the scallion into thin strips.

❷Heat the sauce ingredients in a small pot, and cook them until thick.

❸Cut the tofu into 6 portions, and place it on a plate. Top it with the octopus and seaweed mixture, and pour the sauce over.

KOCHUJAN

Kochujan is chili miso, one of the typical Korean seasonings. The main ingredients are glutinous rice powder or wheat flour mixed with malted beans, chili powder, and salt. The taste and acidity vary according to the ingredients. It is used as a sauce for broiled meat, bibimbap and fried foods.

°°SHOYU SAUCE

Crunchy vegetables covered with Korean-style sauce.

O Ingredients

1 cake silken tofu
50 g (1¾ oz) bean sprouts
⅓ cucumber
Dash of salt

Sauce

1⅓ Tbsp vinegar
1⅓ Tbsp soy sauce
2 tsp sugar
2 tsp sesame oil
½ minced scallion
Dash of grated garlic
Dash of chili powder
Toasted white sesame seeds
Strips of chili pepper

O Method

❶Cut the cucumber in half lengthwise and then slice it diagonally. Cut away the ends of the bean sprouts and boil them in salted water.

❷Combine the sauce ingredients.

❸Place the tofu on a plate. Top with the vegetables and pour the sauce over. Scatter white sesame seeds over the tofu and put strips of chili pepper on top.

ITALIAN-STYLE YAKKO

◌◌BALSAMIC SAUCE

A delicate contrast between tofu and crispy bacon. Savor the taste of balsamic vinegar.

◯ Ingredients
- 1 cake zaru tofu (see p. 68)
- 1 tomato
- 1 strip of bacon
- 2 stalks of arugula
- Dash of olive oil
- Dash of salt and pepper
- 2 Tbsp balsamic vinegar

◯ Method

❶Cut the tomato in half and then into 6 to 8 wedges. Remove the leaves from the arugula

❷Cut the bacon in half. Heat the olive oil in a frying pan and stir-fry the bacon over low heat until crisp. Transfer it to a paper towel and shred it by hand.

❸Place the tofu in a dish and top with the vegetables and bacon. Sprinkle with salt and pepper and pour balsamic vinegar over.

BALSAMIC VINEGAR

Italian fermented vinegar made from grapes. It has a characteristic dark color and rich sweet-sour taste.
As dressing or sauce, it is indispensable for Italian cooking.
In the past, it was used for medicinal purposes.

⚇ANCHOVY SAUCE

This sauce can be used in many recipes.

O **Ingredients**
1 cake zaru tofu (see p. 68)
3 stalks of asparagus
¼ purple onion
⅙ yellow pepper
Sauce
  ½ Tbsp Dijon mustard
  1 egg yolk
  ½ clove garlic, grated
  Dash of salt
  1 Tbsp vinegar
1 cup olive oil
30 g (1 oz) anchovy

O **Method**
❶Trim off the hard root of the asparagus, and boil it in salted water. Cut into 1 cm (⅜ in) lengths. Cut the onion into thin slices, soak in water, and drain. Dice the yellow pepper into 5mm (⅛ in) pieces..
❷Blend the sauce ingredients together in a blender. Mix well, adding the olive oil gradually. Chop up the anchovy and mix in.
❸Place the tofu in a dish. Top it with the vegetables and pour the sauce over.

ANCHOVY

Anchovies are rarely eaten fresh, and they are usually sold in cans or jars. Anchovy paste in a tube is also available. The tiny fillets, unsalted and packed in oil, have an attractive color.

HOME MADE TOFU

The ingredients of tofu are soybeans, coagulant, and water. Homemade tofu is simple, and you can choose your own ingredients. There are a variety of soybeans and the sizes range from large to small, but medium-sized beans are suitable for tofu. Nigari or bittern is traditionally used as the curdling agent. Since 80% of tofu is water, you should use high-quality water to make ttofu.

WHAT IS NIGARI?

Nigari is the coagulant that solidifies the protein contained in soymilk. It is a by-product that remains after natural sea salt is extracted from sea water. The principal component of nigari is magnesium chloride, and it also contains magnesium sulfate and potassium chloride. Other curdling agents besides nigari are magnesium sulfate and gluconodeltalactone, and they are used according to the types of tofu. The nigari is said to bring out the sweetness of tofu.

INGREDIENTS

300 g (10½ oz) soybeans
1 Tbsp curdling agent
6 cups water

1 Remove and discard any spoiled beans. Wash the rest well in water and drain in a bamboo colander. Put them in a bowl and cover with water equivalent to three times the volume of soybeans. Leave them to soak overnight. Let them stand for 8 to 10 hours in summer and 18 to 20 hours in winter.

2 Soybeans left overnight.

The soaked beans are 2 to 3 times larger than dry ones.

3 Remove the well-soaked soybeans to a bamboo basket and drain. Divide the beans into 2 or 3 parts. Put ⅓ of the beans in a blender and add the same amount of water. Blend well until the mixture is creamy. Continue blending the rest of the beans in. When a blender is not available, use a food processor and crush the beans into small pieces and add water.

4 The soft white liquid obtained from crushed beans and water is called go.

PASTE

Good for canapes at a party. If you wish to make it richer, add more fresh cream.

Ingredients

100 g (3½ oz) okara

Paste

   1 Tbsp inaka-miso (miso made from
   soybeans and barley)

   2 - 3 Tbsp mayonnaise

   2 - 3 Tbsp fresh cream

Coarsely ground black pepper

Orange peppers

Cucumbers

Celery

Method

❶Add the miso, mayonnaise, and fresh cream to the okara, and mix well.

❷Transfer the mixture to a bowl and sprinkle with the black pepper. Garnish with vegetables cut into bite-sized pieces.

CROQUETTES

The preliminary seasoning gives it a Japanese-style flavor.

Ingredients

200 g (7 oz) okara
100 g (3½ oz) ground pork
2 Tbsp salad oil
½ medium carrot
1 scallion

Broth

  1 cup dashi stock
  2 Tbsp sugar
  2½ Tbsp soy sauce
  1 Tbsp sake

1 egg, beaten
Batter
Wheat flour
Beaten egg
Breadcrumbs
Oil for deep-frying

Method

❶Cut the carrot into julienne strips. Cut the scallion into thin round slices.

❷Heat the salad oil in a frying pan, and stir-fry ground pork, carrot, scallion, and okara. Add the broth ingredients and cook until the liquid is absorbed. Remove the pan from the heat, mix in the beaten egg, and let it cool.

❸Shape the mixture into flattened spheres. Dust with flour, dip into beaten egg, and roll in breadcrumbs.

❹Heat the oil to 180℃ (360° F) in a pan, and deep-fry the mixture until golden brown and crisp.

⚇ SALAD

No one would ever guess that the main ingredient is okara.
The delicate texture is like potato salad.

⊙ Ingredients
150 g (5¼ oz) okara
2 slices ham
¼ onion
50 g (1¾ oz) carrot
½ cucumber
Dressing
   2-3 Tbsp mayonnaise
   1 Tbsp vinegar
   ¼ tsp salt
   Dash of pepper
Salt
Mint

⊙ Method
❶Cut the ham, cucumber, carrot into thin strips. Cut the onion into thin slices, rub it with salt, and press out the water.
❷Combine the dressing ingredients and mix in the okara. Add the vegetables and ham and mix well.
❸Transfer the mixture to a bowl and garnish with leaves of mint, if desired.

TOFU AS A MAIN DISH

Tofu is a versatile ingredient, good for simmering, broiling and deep-frying. You can develop your own ideas for turning it into a variety of main dishes.

SIMMERING

BRAISED BEEF AND TOFU

A sukiyaki-style recipe that goes well with boiled rice.
Its appeal lies in its intense flavor.

Ingredients
1 cake momen tofu
100 g (3½ oz) beef
4 shallots
1 pack enoki mushrooms
Broth
   1-1½ cup dashi stock
   1 Tbsp sake
   2½ Tbsp soy sauce
   1 Tbsp mirin
   1 Tbsp sugar

Method
❶Cut the beef into bite-sized chunks.
❷Cut the tofu into eight cubes. Cut the shallots into 5 cm (2 in) lengths. Trim the ends of the enoki mushrooms and break them up.
❸Boil the broth ingredients in a flat-bottomed pot. When it came to a boil, add the beef. When it boils again, add the shallots and enoki mushrooms. Simmer over moderate heat for 3 to 4 minutes until the tofu is cooked.

EEL AND TOFU

Cornstarch thickens the dashi and enhances the taste of the tofu.

◯ Ingredients

1 cake momen tofu
1 skewer of broiled eel

Broth

1-1½ cup dashi stock
1 Tbsp mirin
1 Tbsp light soy sauce
⅕ tsp salt
1 tsp cornstarch
100 g (3½ oz) potherb mustard
Powdered pepper

◯ Method

❶ Cut the tofu into 8 cubes. Cut the broiled eel into bite-sized pieces. Cut the potherb mustard into 5 cm (2 in) lengths.

❷ Boil the broth ingredients in a pot. When it comes to a boil, add the tofu and eel and cook for 5 minutes.

❸ Add the potherb mustard to the broth and boil briefly.

❹ Transfer the mixture to a bowl and sprinkle with powdered pepper, if desired.

⚇YANAGAWA-STYLE TOFU

Yanagawa is a loach stew, but here tofu is used instead of loaches.
Topping it with a soft beaten egg is a nice touch.

⦿ Ingredients
⅔ cake momen tofu
3 stalks asparagus
80 g (2⅘ oz) ground chicken
1 egg
Broth
  ⅓ cup dashi stock
  2 tsp soy sauce
  ½ tsp mirin
  1 tsp sugar
Salt

⦿ Method
❶Lay the tofu in a bamboo colander for 10 to 15 minutes to drain. Dice it into 1 cm (⅜ in) pieces.

❷Cut away the ends of the asparagus and boil them in salted water. Drain them in a bamboo colander and cut them diagonally into 3 cm (1⅛ in) lengths.

❸Beat the egg in a bowl.

❹Pour the broth ingredients into a small pot. Add the chicken and boil, stirring constantly. When it came to a boil add the tofu and boil again.

❺Add the asparagus and stir in the egg, lifting the tofu out so that the egg is under it and bring to a boil again.

BRAISED DEEP-FRIED TOFU AND VEGETABLES

The true Chinese flavor is intensified by the deep-fried tofu.

O Ingredients

2 cakes momen tofu
25 g (⅞ oz) string beans
4 shiitake mushrooms
1 red pepper
Broth
  ¾ chicken stock
  1 Tbsp sake
  1 Tbsp soy sauce
  ½ Tbsp oyster sauce
  ¼ sugar
½ tsp sesame oil
Oil for deep-frying

O Method

❶ Wrap the tofu in cloth and lay it on a cutting board with a light weight on top for about 30 minutes to drain. Cut it into 6 pieces.

❷ Preheat the oil to 180℃ (360° F). Remove the excessive water from the tofu and deep-fry until slightly golden brown.

❸ Remove the strings from the string beans and cut them into 3 cm (1⅛ in) lengths. Trim the ends of the mushrooms and cut them in half diagonally.

❹ Heat the sesame oil in a wok and stir-fry the vegetables. Season with the broth. Add the fried tofu and braise for 7 to 8 minutes.

TOFU CURRY

Salt and pepper the tofu prior to cooking to bring out the curry flavor.

Ingredients

1 cake momen tofu
½ onion
4 small green peppers
10 mushrooms
1 clove garlic
1 piece of fresh ginger
1½ Tbsp wheat flour
1½ Tbsp curry powder
1½ Tbsp salad oil
Salt
Pepper
1 bouillon cube
1 cup water

Method

❶Cut the tofu in half horizontally, and then into 8 pieces. Season with salt and pepper.

❷Heat 1 tablespoon of salad oil in a frying pan and brown the tofu on each side.

❸Cut the onion into fine strips and the small green peppers into 1 cm (⅜ in) lengths. Quarter the mushrooms. Chop the garlic and ginger.

❹Heat 1 tablespoon of salad oil in a pot and add the ginger, garlic, onion, small green pepper, and mushrooms in this order, and stir-fry. Add the wheat flour and curry powder and stir-fry well until the whole becomes smooth.

❺Add ½ teaspoon of salt, water, and the bouillon cube to the pot. When it came to a boil, reduce the heat and cook for 10 minutes. Add the tofu and mix quickly until well seasoned.

POLLACK ROE AND TOFU

Pollack roe floating in broth goes well with mild silken tofu.

Ingredients

1 cake silken tofu
10 scallions
½ pollack roe
1 Tbsp salad oil
1 cup chicken stock
Dash of salt and pepper
2 Tbsp sake
1½ Tbsp dissolved cornstarch (2 parts water and 1 part cornstarch)

Method

❶Cut scallions into 3 cm (1⅛ in) lengths. Sprinkle sake (extra) over the pollack roe.
❷Heat the salad oil in a wok. Add the pollack roe, chicken stock, and scallions and mix well.
❸Add the tofu to the wok, break it up, and mix it in. Add the sake, salt and pepper and bring to a boil.
❹Stir in the dissolved cornstarch gradually. Thicken the mixture, shaking the wok to blend in the cornstarch.

TOFU STEAK

The outside is crisp, and the inside is soft. Eat it soon after frying.

FRYING

SOY SAUCE AND BUTTER

The fragrance of butter and soy sauce will stimulate your appetite.
Enjoy the simple flavors of grated daikon radish and ginger.

O Ingredients

1 cake momen tofu
Dash each of salt and pepper
Wheat flour
½ Tbsp salad oil
2 Tbsp soy sauce
½ Tbsp mirin
1-2 Tbsp butter
100 g (3½ oz) grated daikon radish
1 piece of fresh ginger, grated

O Method

❶Cut the tofu in half horizontally. Wrap it in cloth to drain. Apply salt and pepper and coat it with flour, shaking off the extra flour.
❷Heat the oil in a frying pan and fry the tofu over high heat for about 30 seconds. Reduce heat and cook it over low heat for 1 minute. Turn it over and fry over high heat for about 30 seconds. Reduce the heat and cook it for 1 minute until golden brown.
❸Wipe off the oil of the frying pan and add the soy sauce and mirin. Spread butter on top of the tofu and fry over low heat for 30 seconds. Turn up the heat and cover the tofu with sauce.
❹Transfer the tofu to a container and pour the remaining sauce in the frying pan over it. Top with grated daikon radish and ginger.

TOMATO SAUCE

Tofu steak is very versatile. This dish has an Italian-style tang.

Ingredients

1 cake momen tofu
¼ onion
½ clove garlic
200 g (7 oz) canned tomato
Dash of soy sauce
Salt and pepper
Wheat flour
Dash of oregano
2 basil leaves
1 Tbsp salad oil

Method

❶Cut tofu in half horizontally. Wrap it in cloth and put a light weight on it to drain. Apply salt and pepper and coat with flour, shaking off the extra flour.
❷Heat 2 teaspoon of salad oil in a frying pan and fry the tofu on each side until golden brown. Pour the soy sauce over it.
❸Chop up the onion and garlic. Fry them with 1 teaspoon of salad oil until transparent. Add the tomato, mashing it. Season with ¼ teaspoon of salt and a dash of pepper. Sprinkle with the oregano. When the mixture comes to a boil, reduce the heat and simmer for 5 to 10 minutes, stirring occasionally.
❹Place the tofu on a plate and pour the sauce over. cut the basil into small pieces and sprinkle it over the top.

MUSHROOM SAUCE

The mushrooms evoke autumn, and you can taste a hint of ginger.

Ingredients

1 cake momen tofu
Dash each of salt and pepper
Wheat flour
3 raw shiitake mushrooms
½ pack each of shimeji and enoki mushrooms
¼ yellow pepper
Broth
　⅓ cup chicken stock
　1½ Tbsp each of mirin and sake
　1½ Tbsp soy sauce
　½ Tbsp liquefied ginger
1 Tbsp salad oil
1 Tbsp dissolved cornstarch (2 parts water and 1 part cornstarch)

Method

❶Cut the tofu in half horizontally. Wrap it in cloth and put a light weight on it to drain. Combine the broth ingredients.
❷Slice the shiitake mushrooms leaving a bit of stem. Trim the ends of the shimeji and enoki mushrooms and separate them. Cut the yellow pepper into strips.
❸Season the tofu with salt and pepper. Coat it with flour, shaking off the extra flour.
❹Heat the salad oil in a frying pan and fry the tofu until the surface becomes crispy. Transfer it to a plate.
❺Add the shiitake, shimeji, and enoki mushrooms, and the yellow pepper in this order to the frying pan and stir-fry. Add the broth mixture and dissolved cornstarch and pour the whole mixture over the tofu.

⣿FRIED PORK ROLLS

These hearty and substantial meat rolls will perk you up.

O Ingredients

1 cake momen tofu
8 pieces of meat (pork ribs)
Dash of salt and pepper
½ Tbsp salad oil

Sauce

1 Tbsp soy sauce
1 tsp sugar
1 Tbsp sake
1 tsp doubanjiang (see p. 10)

O Method

❶Wrap the tofu in a paper towel to drain. Cut it into 6 portions.

❷Salt and pepper the meat and wrap it around the tofu pieces.

❸Heat the salad oil in a frying pan and fry the rolls over medium heat with the end of the roll facing down. Continue frying, turning over, until golden brown. Combine the sauce ingredients and pour over the rolls. Keep turning the rolls over, until they are well seasoned with the sauce.

TOFU BROILED WITH SWEET SAUCE

Inspired by the cuisine served in Buddhist monasteries, this dish has a shrimp flavor that takes you by surprise.

Ingredients

1 cake momen tofu
150g (5¼ oz) Japanese yam
Dash of vinegar
¼ tsp salt
15 g (½ oz) small shrimps
2 Tbsp sake
1 sheet nori seaweed
Sauce
  2 Tbsp dashi stock
  2 Tbsp mirin
  2 Tbsp soy sauce
  1-2 Tbsp salad oil

Method

❶Dice the tofu and boil it. Transfer it to a bamboo colander to drain. Sprinkle sake over the shrimp, and allow them to stand for about 10 minutes, and chop them up.

❷Combine the tofu and shrimp in a mortar and grind them well.

❸Peel the yam and soak it in vinegar. Grate it and combine it with the shrimp-tofu mixture. Add salt and mix well.

❹Cut the nori into 8 pieces. Divide the mixture into 8 portions and spread some on each nori sheet.

❺Heat the salad oil in a frying pan and fry the sheets with the nori side up. Turn them over and fry the other side.

❻Add the sauce and spoon it over the sheets as you continue frying them.

CRUMBLY SCRAMBLED TOFU

A popular dish. Squeeze the tofu well so that it is easy to crumble.

FRYING

Ingredients

1 cake momen tofu
50 g (1¾ oz) carrot
50 g (1¾ oz) ground chicken
4 string beans
4-5 tree ears
Dash of salt

Soy sauce mixture

2 tsp sugar
1 Tbsp light-colored soy sauce
1 Tbsp sake
1 medium egg
2 tsp salad oil

Method

❶Soak the tree ears in water. Rise the dirt from the surface, and boil briefly. Cut them into strips.

❷Cut the carrot into 4 cm (1½ in) lengths and into fine strips. Boil the string beans in salted water. Transfer them to water to cool and cut diagonally into thin pieces.

❸Cut the tofu into large cubes and boil briefly in hot water. Transfer it to a cloth-lined bamboo colander. Wrap it in the cloth and break it into small pieces, squeezing out the water.

❹Heat the salad oil in a pan and stir-fry the ground chicken. When it is browned, add the carrot and tree ears in this order and continue stir-frying. When all the ingredients are covered with oil, crumble the tofu into the pan and stir-fry again.

❺Season with the soy sauce mixture, and swirl in the beaten egg. Keep cooking and stirring until the whole mixture becomes crumbly and add the string beans.

FRIED BITTER MELON

A popular dish in Okinawa. When the ingredients are ready, stir-fry with a delicate touch.

⭘ Ingredients

1 cake momen tofu
½ bitter melon
½ tsp salt
1 tsp soy sauce
2 eggs
Salad oil
Sesame oil

⭘ Method

❶Drain the tofu in a bamboo colander.
❷Cut the bitter melon in half lengthwise and remove the seeds. Cut it into 5 mm (⅛ in) widths. Soak the pieces in salted water (1 cup water + 1 Tbsp salt). When they become tender, gently squeeze the water out.
❸Beat the egg in a bowl.
❹Heat the salad oil and sesame oil in a frying pan and stir-fry the bitter melon pieces over medium heat. Add the tofu, breaking it into pieces, and stir-fry over high heat about 1 to 2 minutes. Sprinkle the salt in and swirl the soy sauce in along the side of the pan. Add the eggs and stir-fry.

OYSTERS AND TOFU FRIED WITH OYSTER SAUCE

Oysters and oyster sauce go together paerfectly. A thick and rich dish.

Ingredients

1 cake momen tofu
130 g (4½ oz) oysters
Salt and wheat flour
1 scallion
1 clove garlic
1 piece of fresh ginger
1½ Tbsp salad oil

Broth

1 Tbsp oyster sauce
½ Tbsp sake
½ tsp sugar
1 tsp soy sauce
4 Tbsp chicken broth

Method

❶Rinse the oysters in salted water and drain. Cut the scallion diagonally into thin slices. Cut the garlic and ginger into thin slices.
❷Cut the tofu into 6 to 8 cubes and coat with flour.
❸Heat ½ tablespoon of salad oil in a frying pan, sauté both sides of the tofu. Then remove the tofu from the pan and set it aside.
❹Heat 1 tablespoon of salad oil in the same pan. Coat the oysters with flour and add them. Add the garlic, ginger, and tofu, and season with the broth ingredients. Cook for 3 to 4 minutes.

CRABMEAT AND TOFU FRIED WITH SALT

Simple, unpretentious Chinese home cooking.

Ingredients

1 cake silken tofu
100 g (3½ oz) crabmeat (canned)
1 Tbsp sake
3 stalks bok choy
1 piece of fresh ginger
1 Tbsp salad oil
1⅓ cups chicken stock

Sake mixture

1 Tbsp sake
⅓ tsp salt
Dash of pepper

1½ Tbsp dissolved cornstarch (2 parts water and 1 part cornstarch)

Method

❶Cut the tofu in half horizontally and then into 1 cm (2½ in) widths.
❷Remove the crabmeat from the can and pick out bits of cartilage. Break the meat into pieces and sprinkle sake over it.
❸Cut cut the bok choy into 4 cm (1½ in) widths. Cut the ginger into strips.
❹Heat the salad oil in a wok and stir-fry the bok choy and ginger. Mix in the chicken stock and crabmeat. When the stock came to a boil, shake the wok and mix thoroughly.
❺Add the sake mixture and boil again.
❻Swirl in the dissolved cornstarch. Shake the wok to thicken the mixture.

DEEP-FRYING

⚇HOMEMADE DEEP-FRIED TOFU BALLS

Deep-fried tofu prepared at home tastes great, served hot or cold.

◯ Ingredients
1 cake momen tofu
1 egg
50 g (1¾ oz) ground pork
3 g (⅛ oz) tree ear
25 g (⅞ oz) carrot
8 ginkgo nuts
1 Tbsp cornstarch
Flavorings
  ¾ tsp sake
  ½ tsp each of salt and soy sauce
  ½ tsp liquefied ginger
Oil for deep-frying

◯ Method
❶Boil the tofu in hot water and transfer it to a bamboo coriander. Wrap it in cloth and squeeze out the water.
❷Cut the carrot in strips. Soak the tree ear in water to reconstitute it and cut it into fine strips.
❸Break the tofu into pieces in a bowl and season it with the flavoring ingredients. Add the carrot, tree ear, ground pork, beaten egg, and cornstarch and mix well.
❹Divide the mixture into 8 portions. Shape each potion into a ball and put a ginkgo nut in the middle.
❺Preheat the oil to 175℃ (350˚ F), and deep-fry the tofu balls until the surface turns golden brown.

DEEP-FRIED TOFU ROLLED IN SALMON

Be sure to follow the instructions exactly. This recipe offers you a chance
to show off your culinary skills.

O Ingredients

½ cake momen tofu
2 slices salmon
6 green perilla leaves
Salt
Dash of pepper
2 Tbsp cornstarch
Sauce
  ½ cup dashi stock
  ½ Tbsp soy sauce
  Dash of salt
  1 tsp mirin
Oil for deep-frying

O Method

❶Transfer the tofu to a bamboo colander,
wrap it in cloth and drain. Cut it in half
horizontally and then into three cubes.
Season with salt and pepper.

❷Remove the skin from the salmon slices.
Chill them briefly in the freezer. Cut them into
three slices. Season with salt.

❸Combine the sauce ingredients.

❹Place the perilla leaves on the salmon, roll
the tofu, and fix with toothpicks.

❺Coat one side of the rolls with cornstarch,
and deep-fry in the oil preheated to 180℃
(360° F).

❻Remove toothpicks form the rolls, and
transfer them to a plate. Dip in the sauce
before serving.

CHINESE-STYLE TOFU FRIED WITH BATTER

The Chinese-style batter makes this dish fluffy and crisp, and the huajiaoyan and curry powder give it an appealing spicy flavor.

Ingredients
2 cakes momen tofu
Batter
  2 Tbsp cornstarch
  1 cup wheat flour
  1 tsp baking powder
  ⅓ tsp salt
  ¾ cup water
  2 Tbsp salad oil
Salted curry powder
Huajiaoyan (Sichuan pepper salt)
Oil for deep-frying

Method
❶Combine the batter ingredients and mix well. Stir in the salad oil and allow to stand for 1 hour.
❷Press the tofu gently to remove some of the water and cut it into 8 cubes.
❸Preheat the oil to 180℃ (360° F). Coat the tofu with plenty of batter and deep-fry it.
❹Transfer the tofu to a plate and serve it with salted curry powder and huajiaoyan.

Huajiao (Sichuan peppercorns)
Huajiao has a strong smell and a powerfully sharp and bitter taste. Huajiaoyan is made of ground Sichuan peppercorns mixed with salt and lightly toasted together.

DEEP-FRIED TOFU MARINATED IN VINEGAR

The tofu is fried long enough to make it crisp. Coriander adds a characteristic flavor.

Ingredients
1 cake momen tofu
Wheat flour
Oil for deep-frying
¼ purple onion
1 red chili pepper
Marinade
  ½ cup vinegar
  ¼ cup water
  1 Tbsp sugar
  ½ tsp salt
  1 Tbsp soy sauce
Coriander

Method
❶Wrap the tofu in a dry cloth and press it with a weight to drain. Cut it in half and then into three parts horizontally.
❷Cut the purple onion into thin slices. Seed the red chili pepper and cut it into thin round slices.
❸Combine the marinade ingredients, the onion, and the chili pepper in a large flat container, and mix briefly to make a sauce.
❹Preheat the oil to 165℃ (330° F). Slide the tofu into it. When it comes to the surface, deep-fry it over high heat for about 10 minutes until it is golden brown and crisp.
❺While the tofu is still hot, drop it into the marinade, and marinate it for 30 to 40 minutes. Garnish with the purple onion and coriander and serve.

STEAMING

TOFU WRAPPED IN EGG POUCHES

You will like this lightly steamed variation on a traditional dish with an unusual sauce.

O Ingredients
⅔ cake (200 g (7 oz)) momen tofu
40 g (1½ oz) crab (canned)
1 egg
1 Tbsp green peas (frozen)
1 Tbsp mayonnaise
½ Tbsp milk

O Method
❶ Wrap the tofu in a paper towel and transfer it to a bamboo colander. Press it with a weight to drain and then crush it into small pieces.
❷ Take out the crabmeat out of the can and remove the bits of cartilage. Break the meat into pieces. Defrost the green peas by boiling briefly and then drain them.
❸ Beat the egg in a bowl. Mix in the crushed tofu and add salt and the peas and crabmeat. Mix well.
❹ Line a small container with plastic wrap. Place ¼ portion of the mixture in it, fold it into a pouch, twist the mouth, and secure it with a rubber band. Repeat with each portion of the mixture.
❺ Arrange the pouches in a plate, place them in an already steaming steamer and steam for 7 to 8 minutes.
❻ Allow the pouches to cool in the plastic wrap. Then remove the wrap and transfer them to a bowl to serve.
❼ Thin the mayonnaise with the milk and spoon it over the pouches.

:::STEAMED SALMON AND TOFU

The sauce and chili oil bring about the sweetness of the salmon and tofu.

○ Ingredients

1 cake momen tofu
4 Tbsp salmon flakes
60 g (2 oz) ground chicken
¼ scallion
1 small egg

Seasonings

⅓ tsp salt
1½ Tbsp sake
1 tsp ginger juice

1½ Tbsp cornstarch
3 string beans

Sauce

Soy sauce
Sesame oil
Chili oil

○ Method

❶Wrap the tofu in a paper towel and transfer it to a bamboo colander. Press it with a weight to drain. Chop up the scallion. Boil the string beans and cut them into 1 cm (⅜ in) lengths.

❷Combine the ground chicken, scallion, beaten egg and seasonings in a bowl and mix well. Add the crumbled tofu, salmon flakes, string beans, and cornstarch, and mix well.

❸Transfer the mixture to a container and pat down the surface. Put it in a preheated steamer and steam over high heat for 15 minutes. (When using a microwave oven, cover with plastic wrap and heat for 6 to 7 minutes.)

❹Combine the sauce ingredients and swirl them over the top. You may use sour orange juice instead, if desired.

°TOFU TOPPED WITH STEAMED SHRIMP

Lovely, ingeniously-constructed bite-sized pieces.

O Ingredients
⅔ cake silken tofu
100 g (3½ oz) shelled shrimp
(A) ½ egg white
    ½ Tbsp sake
    ½ Tbsp cornstarch
    Dash of salt
Cornstarch
Coriander
Sauce
    ½ Tbsp soy sauce
    ½ tsp sesame oil

O Method
❶Devein the shrimp , crush, and combine with the (A) ingredients.
❷Wrap the tofu in a paper towel and drain. Cut it into 8 cubes and arrange it in a heatproof dish.
❸Dust the tofu with cornstarch, and top each of the 8 cubes of tofu with ⅛ of the shrimp mixture.
❹Place the cubes in a pre-heated steamer, and steam for 6 to 7 minutes.
❺Garnish the cubes with coriander, and pour the sauce ingredients over them.

COD WITH TOFU & VEGETABLES

This simple but attractive dish will never fail to please your guests.

Ingredients

½ cake momen tofu
2 fillets cod
⅕ tsp salt
Dash of sake
2 7 cm (2½ in) squares of kombu
30 g (1 oz) garland chrysanthemum leaves
20 g (⅔ oz) enoki mushrooms

Flavoring sauce

⅓ cup dashi stock
1 tsp soy sauce
½ tsp mirin
Citron peel

Method

❶Cut the cod in half, and sprinkle with salt and sake. Allow to stand for 10 minutes.

❷Wipe the kombu with a wet cloth. Pluck the soft part of the chrysanthemum leaves. Remove the stem base of the enoki mushrooms and break them into pieces. Transfer the tofu into a bamboo colander to drain.

❸Spread the kombu in a container and arrange the tofu, cod, and enoki on top of it divided into equal parts. Pour the flavoring sauce over it.

❹Place the container in a pre-heated steamer. When steam rises again, steam over medium heat for 10 to 12 minutes. (When using a microwave oven, cover the container with plastic wrap and heat for 60 to 90 seconds per portion.)

❺During the steaming process, lift the lid and top the ingredients with chrysanthemum leaves, and then replace the lid and allow to stand for 30 seconds.

❻Remove the portions from the steamer and serve topped with a slice of citron peel.

VARIETIES OF TOFU

Tofu is classified by manufacturing method and size. The name "tofu" comes from the Chinese dou-fu. *Dou* means "soybean" in Chinese, while *fu* refers to a lump or a soft solid. The name is therefore an apt one, in terms of both its nature and its history.

MOMEN TOFU
(Cotton Tofu / Regular Tofu)

The name is said to come from the surface markings left by the weave of the cotton cloth in which the tofu is formed. It is sometimes called regular tofu. It has softer and a more delicate texture than Chinese-style "firm tofu," which has a meaty texture.

To make momen tofu, begin by soaking soybeans in water until they become soft. Grind the beans and separate the soymilk from the lees. Add bittern to curdle the tofu. Pour it into a mold with cloth spread over the holes in the bottom. Cover the whole thing with another cloth and place a bamboo mat on it. Put weight on top and drain the extra water. When it is firm, remove it from the mold in a large container of water. Store it in the water.

Momen tofu contains less water than other kinds of tofu, and it is highly nutritious. It is full of nutrients such as proteins, lipids, calcium, iron, and phosphorus.

SOFT TOFU

Soft tofu is made from the soymilk the thickness of which is between that used for momen tofu and silken tofu. The process of making it is the same as for momen tofu. It is softer than momen tofu and feels smooth on the tongue.

JUTEN TOFU (Stuffed Tofu)

Juten tofu is made by a method developed within the past fifty or sixty years. Soymilk and curdling agent are stuffed together in a pack or tubular bag. The sealed package is heated to firm the tofu. The thickness of soymilk is the same as that used for silken tofu, and the result has a similar texture. It is smooth like kinugoshi tofu. Since juten tofu is not exposed to water and is heated only after being packed, it is characterized by an especially high level of vitamin B1, which is easily destroyed by water and heat. However, it contains less protein, lipid, and calcium than momen and silken tofu.

YOSE TOFU (Gathered Tofu)

Soymilk begins to curdle when coagulant is added. The half-curdled tofu is scooped into a bowl or pail without being formed into blocks like momen or silken tofu. This is yose tofu. It has a soft texture. (See p. 37)

OBORO TOFU (Hazy Tofu)

The half-curdled tofu scooped into water and drained. It has an indistinct form. The term also refers to a ball of tofu which is boiled and covered with a paste of arrowroot starch. It looks like the moon on a hazy evening.

ZARU TOFU (Colander Tofu)

This type of tofu is put into a bamboo colander and left to drain naturally. It has a rich taste. (See p. 37)

SILKEN TOFU

Silken tofu is made from soymilk thicker than that used for momen tofu. The soymilk used for momen tofu has ten parts water to one part soybeans, while the soymilk used for silken tofu has only five parts water to one part soybeans. After bittern is added, the soymilk is poured into a mold without holes. A lid is placed on the mold, and it is allowed to stand until the soymilk is curdled. Unlike the process for momen tofu, no cloth is used, so the surface of silken tofu has no marks of cloth. The feel of silken tofu in the mouth is soft and smooth. As the water is not drained, it is soft and fragile. Along with the retained water, it contains a high concentration of water-soluble vitamins.

A BRIEF HISTORY OF TOFU

The firsts tofu was made in China about 2000 years ago.

It was first introduced to Japan in the Nara period (710-784).

It was introduced to Okinawa through trade with China.

It is said that Korean tofu makers immigrated to Tosa on the island of Shikoku.

Tofu was popular as a vegetarian meal among priests in the Kamakura period (1192-1333).

It was first called okabe "wall", and described in cookbooks as kabe or shirakabe "white wall".

The name 'tofu' came to be used in the Muromachi period (1336-1573).

It became popular among the general public in the Edo period (1603-1867).

Tofu is now one of the most popular foods and solidly positioned as one of the basic foods of Japanese cuisine.

THE NUTRITIONAL VALUE OF TOFU

It is well known that soybeans are highly nutritious, and tofu is one of the major food products produced from them. It contains a lot of substances that are essential for human health. Some of the nutrients of soybeans are difficult to absorb, but those of tofu are easily absorbed, so it is an appropriate food for sick persons, aged people, and young children.

PROTEINS

Proteins are the main nutrient in tofu. Proteins build up cells, skin, internal organs, muscles, bones, and blood and are also components of enzymes and hormones. Tofu contains a large quantity of nutritious, high-quality proteins, which are broken down into amino acids and absorbed in the body. Eight essential amino acids are found in food, and the essential amino acid makeup of a food protein determines its nutritive value. Proteins from soybeans are almost as good as proteins from animal sources, but they lack the high concentrations of cholesterol found in meat. The proteins in tofu lower the cholesterol level in blood, and the peptides reduce blood pressure. Tofu helps to drive down bad cholesterol and decrease total blood cholesterol.

LECITHIN

The word 'lecithin' comes from Greek lekithos "egg yolk." It is found in egg yolks, soybeans, liver, small fish, cereals and sesame oil. The human body consists of about 60 trillion of cells, each of which is covered by a membrane made up mostly of lecithin. It is approximately one percent of the body weight. The lecithin dissolves the cholesterol that adheres to the blood vessels and keeps blood flowing smoothly. It is therefore effective in preventing hardening of the arteries and myocardial infarctions. Inositol, one of the components of lecithin, is essential to the growth of skin and hair. It improves the circulation of the blood in the brain and promotes new hair growth. It also helps to prevent cirrhosis of the liver by preventing fat from being deposited in the liver.

CHOLINE

Choline, one of the constituents of lecithin, is effective in promoting brain activity. Lecithin itself is an important constituent of nerve cells. Lecithin is decomposed into choline in the intestines. The choline changes into acetylcholine in the brain and plays an important role in developing memory and powers of concentration. It also prevents senility.

SAPONIN

The main constituent of the bubbles that rise to the surface when adzuki beans and soybeans are boiled is saponin. By itself, it has a harsh, unpleasant aftertaste. Saponin is one of the glycosides, compounds of sugar and other substances. In the body, it controls the formation of peroxide, which causes the hardening of the arteries, and reduces cholesterol and natural fat. It also prevents the oxidation of a fatty acid that promotes aging. It is effective in preventing constipation and warding off a hangover. Research is currently under way to investigate reports that saponin may be effective in preventing cancer and AIDS.

ISOFLAVONE

Isoflavones have recently attracted worldwide attention. Like saponin, insoflavonoids are glycosides, and no food contains higher concentrations of them than soybeans. The reason these substances have attracted attention is that their action within the body is similar to that of the female hormone estrogen. Since estrogen controls the deposition of calcium in the body, its ability to prevent osteoporosis has been noted, along with it ability to alleviate the symptoms of menopause.

CALCIUM

Calcium is responsible for the hardness of bones and teeth and plays an important role in regulating normal physiology. A lack of calcium can make us oversensitive and overly irritable. The high-quality protein of tofu is said to promote the otherwise difficult absorption of calcium.

OLIGOSACCHARIDES

Oligosaccharides are the type of carbohydrate that makes tofu sweet. They nourish beneficial bifidobacteria in the colon and improve the balance of intestinal bacteria. They are indigestible, and when they reach the colon, they inhibit the growth of harmful bacteria, boost the immune function, and prevent cancer of the large intestine. Low in energy, they stabilize blood sugar levels and improve the absorption of calcium. Tofu has little fiber, but like other vegetable fibers, it helps clean out the intestines.

VITAMINS

Tofu does not have as many vitamins as soybeans, since heat is used in the process of making it. However, it contains vitamins E, B1, B2, and niacin. Vitamin E improves the circulation of the blood and is effective in clearing the skin, relieving stiffness of the shoulders and low back pain. It is said to be an anti-oxidant, helpful in preventing cancer and chronic lifestyle diseases. The B vitamins keep the skin and mucous membranes healthy, and the niacin maintains the condition of the skin and digestive tract.

HOMEMADE ABURAGE AND ATSUAGE

Try making aburage (tofu pouches) and atsuage (tofu cutlets) at home.
Make them smaller than the storebought varieties, so that they will be easier to deep-fry. Take your time preparing them, and enjoy the result.

HOMEMADE ABURAGE
(Homemade Tofu Pouches)

Ingredients

1 cake momen tofu
Oil for deep-frying

Method

1 Drain the tofu with a weight on it. Cut it horizontally into 7 mm (¼ in)- thick slices.
2 Preheat the oil to 165℃ (330° F). Slide the tofu in and deep-fry it over medium heat.
3 When the tofu comes up to the surface, turn the flame up to high and deep-fry until the pouches are crisp and golden brown. The cooking time is 10 to 12 minutes.

BAKED SCALLION AND MISO

Scallions go well with miso. This is a good accompaniment to drinks.

Ingredients

6 homemade aburage (made of 1 cake of tofu)
5 cm (2 in) scallion
Topping
  1 Tbsp inaka miso (salty miso made with barley)
  1 tsp sake
  1 tsp mirin

Method

1 Cut the scallion into thin round slices.
2 Combine the topping ingredients in a bowl. Add the scallion slices and mix well.
3 Spread the topping on the surface of the aburage, and bake it in a toaster oven for 1 to 2 minutes.

GINGER AND SOY SAUCE

A familiar combination that enhances the flavor of homemade aburage.

Ingredients

6 pieces homemade aburage (corresponds to 1 cake of tofu)
Grated fresh ginger
Soy sauce

Method

Put the grated ginger on top of the deep-fried hot aburage, and pour soy sauce over it.

HOMEMADE ATSUAGE
(Homemade Tofu Cutlets)

Ingredients

1 cake momen tofu
Oil for deep-frying

Method

1 Drain the tofu with a weight on it. Cut it in half.
2 Preheat the oil to 165℃ (330° F). Slide the tofu in and deep-fry it over medium heat.
3 When the tofu comes up to the surface, turn the flame up to high and deep-fry until the cutlets are crisp and golden brown. The cooking time is about 12 minutes.

Deep-fry over high heat, turning over occasionally.

Cooked through with a golden brown surface.

CREAMY STEW WITH MISO

A mix of Japanese and Western style stews, suitable for winter.

Ingredients

Homemade atsuage made of 1 cake of tofu
½ onion
2 turnips
30 g (1 oz) turnip leaves
½ carrot
1 Tbsp butter
2 cups broth (made from 1 bouillon cube)
2 Tbsp miso
⅔ cup milk
Dash of salt and pepper

Method

1 Cut the atsuage into 4 cubes. Cut the onion into wedges, 1 cm (⅜ in) thick. Trim the leaves from the turnip, leaving a little stem. Peel the turnip and quarter. Peel the carrot and cut it into round slices, 1 cm (⅜ in) thick.
2 Heat the butter in a pot and stir-fry the onion and carrot until tender.
3 Add the turnip and broth and simmer over low heat for 6 to 7 minutes.
4 Add the atsuage and miso and cook for another 2 to 3 minutes.
5 When the turnip is tender, add the milk and season with salt and pepper.
6 Boil the turnip leaves and cut them into pieces, 3 cm (1⅛ in) long. Add them to the stew and turn off the heat.

SIMPLE ACCOMPANIMENTS TO DRINKS

When all you need is something to go with drinks, simple recipes like these are best. Of course, they can also double as side dishes.

JAPANESE-STYLE TOFU SALAD

O Ingredients
1 cake momen tofu
30 g (1 oz) takuan (pickled daikon radish)
½ cucumber
1 Tbsp white sesame seeds
Flavorings
  ½ – 1 soy sauce
  ½ tsp sugar
  ¼ tsp salt

O Method
❶Drain the tofu in a bamboo colander. Wrap it in a paper towel to expel excess moisture.
❷Chop up the takuan and cucumber. Toast the white sesame seeds.
❸Break up the tofu in a bowl. Combine the flavorings and mix in. Add the takuan and cucumber and mix well.

CHINESE-STYLE TOFU SALAD

O Ingredients
1 cake silken tofu
40 g (1⅖ oz) zhacai (Sichuan pickles) (see p. 86)
1 pidan (preserved duck egg) (see p. 24)
1 red pepper
1-2 stalks coriander
Flavorings
  2 tsp sesame oil
  1 tsp soy sauce
  Dash of salt

O Method
❶Drain the tofu in a bamboo colander. Wrap it in a paper towel to expel excess moisture.
❷Cut the zhacai into thin slices and soak them in water for about 10 minutes to remove the salt. Chop them into coarse pieces. Shell the pidan and cut it into chunks. Remove the stem and seeds from the pepper and chop it into coarse pieces. Chop up the coriander.
❸Break up the tofu in a bowl. Combine the flavorings and mix in. Add the zhacai, pepper, and coriander and mix well.

⣿TOFU SALAD

These recipes are different from usual salads and dressings.
The combinations of ingredients give each of them a highly individual taste.

STANDARD RECIPE

O Ingredients

½ cake momen tofu
50 g (1¾ oz) carrot
½ block konnyaku

(A)
  1 cup dashi stock
  2 Tbsp sake
  2 Tbsp sugar
  1 Tbsp light-colored soy sauce
100 g (3½ oz) spinach

(B)
  ½ Tbsp soy sauce
  ½ Tbsp dashi stock
3 Tbsp toasted white sesame seeds
(or 2 Tbsp sesame paste)

(C)
  1 Tbsp sugar
  ½ Tbsp sake
  ½ - 1 light-colored soy sauce
  ¼ tsp salt

O Method

❶Cut the tofu into appropriate sizes and boil it in hot water. Transfer it to a bamboo colander lined with a dishtowel and lightly squeeze out excess water.

❷Cut the carrot and konnyaku into thin strips.

❸Put the ingredients listed under (A) in a pot and bring them to a boil. Add the carrot and konnyaku strips and simmer.

❹Boil the spinach in salted water, transfer it to fresh water, and squeeze out the excess water. Cut it into pieces, 3 cm (1⅛ in) long, and season with the ingredients listed under (B).

❺Put the sesame seeds in an earthenware mortar, add the tofu, and grind together until smooth. Mix in the ingredients listed under (C), and adjust the thickness with extra dashi stock.

❻Add ❸ and ❹ to ❺, and toss the whole lightly.

VARIATION

O Ingredients

½ cake momen tofu
1 rasher bacon
½ green pepper
60 g (2 oz) burdock root
½ Tbsp sesame oil

(A)
  ½ Tbsp soy sauce
  ½ Tbsp sake
  ½ tsp sugar
2 Tbsp sesame seed paste

(B)
  1 Tbsp sugar
  ½ Tbsp sake
  ½-1 light-colored soy sauce
  ¼ tsp salt

O Method

❶Cut the tofu into appropriate sizes and boil it in hot water. Transfer it to a bamboo colander lined with a dishtowel and lightly squeeze.

❷Cut the bacon into pieces, 1 cm (⅜ in) wide. Cut the green pepper and burdock root into fine strips.

❸Heat the sesame oil in a pan, stir-fry the bacon, burdock, and pepper in that order, and season with the ingredients listed under (A).

❹Put the sesame seeds in an earthenware mortar, add the tofu, and grind together until smooth. Mix in the ingredients listed under (B), and adjust the thickness with extra dashi stock.

❺Add all the ingredients together, and toss them lightly.

⦾WHITE DRESSING

White dressing sauce with tofu and white sesame seeds. The main
ingredients are vegetables.

STANDARD RECIPE

O Ingredients

1 cake momen tofu
1½ Tbsp sesame seed paste
(A)
  1⅓ Tbsp sugar
  ½ tsp salt
  1⅔ Tbsp vinegar
2-3 Tbsp dashi stock
1 cucumber
Dash of salt
80 g (2⅘ oz) shelled shrimp
(B)
  ½ Tbsp vinegar
  Dash of sugar
4 g (⅛ oz) tree ear
(C)
  ½ cup dashi stock
  1 tsp soy sauce

O Method

❶Cut the tofu into appropriate sizes and boil it in water. Transfer it to a bamboo colander lined with a dishtowel and squeeze hard.
❷Grind the tofu in an earthenware mortar. Add the sesame seed paste and the ingredients listed under (A) and adjust the thickness with the dashi stock.
❸Cut the cucumber into round slices and sprinkle them with salt. When it softens, squeeze the moisture out.
❹Devein the shrimp and boil. Cut them in half and season with the ingredients listed under (B).
❺Soak the tree ear in water. Simmer in the ingredients listed under (C) for 1 to 2 minutes. Cut them into strips.
❻Expel the excess moisture from the cucumber, shrimp, and tree ear and dress with the tofu mixture.

VARIATION

O Ingredients

1 cake momen tofu
4 slices smoked salmon
5 cherry tomatoes
2 stalks of asparagus
¼ zucchini
1½ Tbsp sesame seeds past
Flavorings
  1⅓ Tbsp sugar
  ½ tsp salt
  1⅔ Tbsp vinegar
  1 Tbsp juice of lemon
2-3 Tbsp dashi stock

O Method

❶Cut the tofu into appropriate sizes and boil it in water. Transfer it to a bamboo colander lined with a dishtowel and squeeze hard.
❷Grind the tofu in an earthenware mortar. Add the sesame seed paste and the flavorings, and adjust the thickness with dashi stock.
❸Boil the asparagus in water, and cut it into pieces, 2 cm (¾ in) long. Cut the zucchini in half lengthwise and then into thin slices. Sprinkle it with salt. When it softens, squeeze the moisture out. Cut the cherry tomatoes in half after removing the stems. Cut the smoked salmon into pieces, 1 cm (⅜ in) wide.
❹Dress the salmon and vegetables with the tofu mixture.

⚪WHITE DRESSING WITH VINEGAR

A dressing should never be watering. A little care in preparation can have a major effect on the results.

FAST, SIMPLE RECIPES

TOFU DRESSED WITH THICK SAUCE

An elegant recipe ideal for entertaining guests. Don't stint on the sauce.

Ingredients
1 cake silken tofu
Flavorings
　1 cup dashi stock
　1 Tbsp soy sauce
　1 Tbsp mirin
　3 Tbsp dissolved cornstarch (2 parts water and 1 part cornstarch)
Wasabi (Japanese horseradish)
Kombu, 10-15 cm (4 - 6 in) long

Method
❶Put the kombu and tofu in a pot with water and heat.
❷Combine the flavoring ingredients in a small pot and bring to a boil. Skim the scum as it rises and thicken the liquid with dissolved cornstarch.
❸Ladle the tofu into a bowl and pour the sauce over it. Top with the wasabi.

⊗SCALLION AND TOFU COOKED IN SOY SAUCE

A simple, old-fashioned, salty-sweet taste. The flavor of garlic stimulates the appetite.

◯ Ingredients
1 cake momen tofu
1 scallion
1 clove garlic
1 Tbsp salad oil
Flavorings
  4 Tbsp soy sauce
  1 Tbsp sake
  1 tsp sugar

◯ Method
❶Drain the tofu in a bamboo colander. Cut it in half horizontally and then into halves.
❷Cut the scallion diagonally into slices, 8 mm (¼ in) wide. Cut the garlic into thin slices.
❸Heat the salad oil in a pan and stir-fry the garlic and scallion. Add the tofu and stir-fry briefly. Add the flavorings and simmer over low heat for 3 to 4 minutes, shaking the pan and occasionally spooning the liquid over the tofu.

⦂TOFU JON

A typical Korean dish, often prepared for New Year celebrations.

○ Ingredients

1 cake momen tofu
1 egg

Flavorings

   1½ Tbsp soy sauce
   1 clove garlic, grated
   5 cm (2 in) scallion, chopped
   ¼ tsp powdered chili pepper
   ½ tsp sesame seeds, toasted and ground
Dash of salt and pepper
Wheat flour
½ - 1 Tbsp salad oil
½ - 1 Tbsp sesame oil
Strips of chili pepper

○ Method

❶Drain the tofu well. Place it on a bamboo mat and heat it in a microwave oven for 5 minutes.

❷Break the egg in a bowl and beat it.

❸Combine the flavorings to make sauce.

❹Cut the tofu into 7 mm (¼ in)-thick-slices (7-8 pieces from a cake). Coat lightly with wheat flour, salt, and pepper.

❺Heat the salad oil and sesame oil in a frying pan. Dip the tofu in the beaten egg, and fry on both sides over medium heat, topped with strips of chili pepper, for 20 to 30 seconds each.

❻Transfer the hot tofu to a plate and pour the sauce over it.

POT STICKERS

Once you get a taste of this soft pot sticker, you will be hooked. The flavor of dried shrimp adds a fresh ocean-like flavor.

O Ingredients

1 cake momen tofu
1 pack pot sticker skins
40 g (1⅖ oz) dried shrimp
½ scallion
1 piece of fresh ginger
40 g (1⅖ oz) string beans

Flavorings
  ½ tsp salt
  ½ tsp sugar
  1 tsp soy sauce
  Dash of pepper
Salad oil

O Method

❶ Wrap the tofu in a paper towel, drain, and crush.

❷ Chop up the scallion and ginger. Boil the string beans and cut into thin round slices. Soak the dried shrimp in warm water and chop up.

❸ Put the tofu, scallion, ginger, and shrimp into a bowl and mix well. Add the flavorings and mix again.

❹ Divide the mixture into equal portions and wrap it in pot sticker skins.

❺ Heat the salad oil in a frying pan and fry the pot stickers, covered with a lid, over medium heat until they are golden brown and crisp.

TOFU AND ZASAI FRIED WITH MISO

An original recipe that will be prepared quickly. The salty zhacai will stimulate the appetite.

ZASAI

Zasai is a mustard-like tuber, and its pickled form is a well-known part of the cuisine of China's Sichuan province. After being peeled and dried in the shade, it is partially pickled in distilled liquor and salt. It is then drained, sprinkled with salt and chili peppers, placed in a jar, and buried underground to ferment. The salt is rinsed off before it is used in cooking.

Ingredients

1 cake momen tofu
30 g (1 oz) zasai (pickled mustard tuber)
20 g (⅔ oz) nira (Chinese chives)
Fresh ginger
Garlic
1 Tbsp salad oil
½ cup chicken stock

Flavorings
2 tsp red miso
1 Tbsp soy sauce
½ Tbsp sugar
1 Tbsp sake

Method

❶ Cut the tofu into 2 cm (¾ in) cubes. Drop it into boiling water briefly and drain it in a bamboo colander. Cut zasai in half and then into thin slices. Soak it in water for 10 to 15 minutes to desalt. Chop up the ginger and garlic. Cut the nira into pieces, 4 cm (1½ in) long.

❷ Combine the flavorings and mix well.

❸ Heat the salad oil in a wok and stir-fry the garlic and ginger. When you can smell them, add the drained zasai and stir-fry. Add the tofu and nira and briefly stir-fry. Add the chicken stock and the rest of the ingredients. When it comes to a boil, toss the ingredients in the wok to bring them up from the bottom and simmer for 1 to 2 minutes.

TOFU BOILED IN SOY SAUCE WITH GINGER

The flavor and color of soy sauce set off this simmered tofu.

Ingredients
1 cake momen tofu
1 piece of fresh ginger
Flavorings
 1 Tbsp sake
 1 Tbsp mirin
 2½ Tbsp soy sauce
 1 Tbsp sugar
1 Tbsp sesame oil

Method
❶Wrap the in a paper towel and drain. Cut it into 2 cm (¾ in) cubes.
❷Cut the ginger into julienne strips.
❸Heat the sesame oil in a pan and stir-fry the ginger. Add the tofu and the flavorings, and simmer, stirring until the liquid has almost entirely evaporated.

TOFU DRESSED WITH VINEGARED MISO

The combination of tofu and vinegared miso is a refreshing surprise, and Chinese mustard adds a touch of spiciness.

Ingredients
1 cake momen tofu
1 bundle chives
25 g (7/8 oz) salted wakame seaweed
40 g (1 2/5 oz) inaka miso (salty miso made with barley)
1 1/2 Tbsp sugar
1 Tbsp dashi stock
1 1/3 Tbsp vinegar
1/2 tsp Chinese mustard paste

Method
❶Drain the tofu in a bamboo colander. Shred it into bite-size pieces.
❷Boil the bundle of chives briefly and drain. When it is cool, cut it into pieces, 3 cm (1 1/3 in) long. Desalt the wakame seaweed by rinsing it. Boil it briefly in hot water and then transfer to cold water. Remove the strings and cut into pieces, 3 cm (1 1/8 in) long.
❸Mix the miso and sugar. Add the dashi stock, and when it becomes sticky, add the mustard paste and mix well.
❹Place the solid ingredients on a plate, and dress them with the vinegared miso.

TOFU FRIED WITH MISO AND CHEESE

The savory aroma of cheese suggests potatoes au gratin. Eat this piping hot.

Ingredients
1 cake momen tofu
Dash of salt and pepper
Wheat flour
40 g (1 2/5 oz) Mozzarella cheese
Flavorings
 2 Tbsp miso
 1 Tbsp sugar
 1/2 Tbsp dashi stock
 2 Tbsp sake
2 tsp salad oil
30 g (1 oz) broccoli

Method
❶Drain the tofu in a bamboo colander. Cut it into 4 cubes. Coat it with wheat flour and sprinkle with salt and pepper. Break the broccoli into florets and boil.
❷Combine the flavorings and place them in microwave-safe container. Heat them in a microwave for about 50 seconds to 1 minute to make miso paste.
❸Heat the salad oil in a frying pan and fry both sides of the tofu.
❹Place the tofu and broccoli in a microwave-safe dish. Spread the miso paste over them and top with cheese. Heat them in the microwave until the cheese is melted.

PRESERVED TOFU

Once you try preserved tofu, you will be addicted to its taste. It is easy to use and keeps for a long time. You should have it always on hand, because it is useful when you need one more dish.

⦙TOFU PRESERVED IN SOY SAUCE WITH GARLIC

This will stimulate your appetite. You may cut it in strips and place it on top of cooked rice.

⦙TOFU PRESERVED IN MISO

This is tasty even when fermented longer than usual. Coat it with plenty of miso.

⊙ Ingredients
1 cake momen tofu
Flavorings
  ½ cup soy sauce
  2 Tbsp sake
  1 clove garlic, thinly sliced

⊙ Method
❶Wrap the tofu in a paper towel and transfer it to a bamboo colander to drain.
❷Cut the tofu into halves and put it into a container that can be closed tightly. Combine the flavorings and pour them over the tofu. Keep the container in the refrigerator for a day.
※The container should be large enough so that the tofu is just covered with the flavorings. It should be eaten within a week.

⊙ Ingredients
1 cake momen tofu
200 g (7 oz) white miso
35 g (1⅙ oz) red miso
3 Tbsp sake
3 Tbsp mirin

⊙ Method
❶Wrap the tofu in a paper towel and transfer it to a bamboo colander to drain.
❷Combine the white and red miso. Add the sake and mirin and mix well. Put half the mixture in an airtight container.
❸Wrap the tofu in cheesecloth and put it in the container. Spread the rest of the miso mixture over it. Cover the container with its lid and keep it in the refrigerator for three days.
※It should be eaten within 10 days.

⚬ TOFU PRESERVED IN HERB OIL

The Mediterranean seasonings give the tofu a flavor similar to feta cheese.

⚬ TOFU PRESERVED WITH KOCHUJANG

Kochujang is a versatile Korean seasoning made from hot ground chili peppers mixed with mashed beans. It can be used in hot pot dishes.

O Ingredients
1 cake momen tofu
$\frac{1}{2}$ tsp salt
$\frac{2}{3}$ - 1 cup olive oil
Seasonings
  1 bay leaf
  1 sprig rosemary
  1 tsp berries of pepper

O Method
❶Wrap the tofu in a paper towel and transfer it to a bamboo colander to drain.
❷Cut the tofu into 9 cubes and dust it with salt all over.
❸Put the tofu in a jar, and add the seasonings and the olive oil. Keep it in the refrigerator for a day.
※The jar should be large enough so that the tofu is just covered with olive oil. It should be eaten within a week.

O Ingredients
1 cake momen tofu
Flavorings
  5 Tbsp kochujang
  3$\frac{1}{2}$ Tbsp sake
  1$\frac{1}{2}$ Tbsp soy sauce

O Method
❶Wrap the tofu in a paper towel and transfer it to a bamboo colander to drain.
❷Cut the tofu into 9 cubes and put it in a jar.
❸Combine the flavorings. Add them to the jar, which should be refrigerated for half a day.
※It should be eaten within a week.

DRAINING TOFU

Draining is a very important step in cooking tofu. Depending on the method of cooking, the water content of tofu can have a major effect on its taste. There are several ways to drain tofu. Choose the method most appropriate to the recipe.

THE NATURAL WAY WITH A BAMBOO COLANDER

Place a flat bamboo colander on a deep dish or bowl. Put the tofu on it and leave it until the water is drained out. The draining time depends on the amount of the water. You may also place the tofu on a tilted plate or chopping board.

If you want to serve chilled tofu, wrap it in plastic wrap and store it in the refrigerator.

USING ABSORBENT PAPER

When you don't have much time or want to drain the tofu quickly, use commercially available absorbent paper.

Drain the tofu according to the instructions on the package.

WEIGHTING

Wrap the tofu in a paper towel, and place it on a flat surface like an upside down tray or a chopping board with a weight on top. To distribute the weight equally, place a flat object on top as if sandwiching the tofu. You can adjust the amount of drainage by varying the weight.

The water will flow out faster if you fix the bottom surface at a slant.

SHREDDING AND BOILING

If your cooking requires crumbled tofu, break it into pieces before boiling.

If you break the tofu into small pieces, you can drop it into hot water without much splashing.

BOILING

Put tofu and water in a pot and bring them to a boil. Remove the tofu in a bamboo basket and drain it. If you start with cold water, you don]t have to worry about burning your hand, and the tofu retains its original form. Merely heating the tofu like this drains it sufficiently.

If you want the tofu to retain its shape, boil one block or cut it in half.

IN A MICROWAVE OVEN

You can drain tofu by heating it in a microwave oven for the same effect as draining boiled tofu. Place the tofu on a microwave-safe draining tray, and heat 3 minutes for each block of tofu. If no such tray is available, use a heatproof plate with a bamboo screen on it. Instead of a bamboo screen, you may also use a few disposable wooden chopsticks.

When using a microwave oven, heat the tofu without plastic warp.

PRESERVING TOFU

If you preserve tofu properly, you can enjoy it for a long time. The length of time depends on the methods used. Be sure to preserve it in the most appropriate method for its intended use.

Put the tofu in a deep bowl, cover it with water, and store it in the refrigerator. If you don't eat it immediately, change the water once in the morning and once in the evening, and you will be able to keep it for two or three days. This is the best way of preserving leftovers. Tofu loses its flavor as time goes by, but you can still find ways to make it tasty. You can serve fresh tofu chilled and day-old tofu boiled, stewed, or deep-fried. Ordinary tofu in a package will keep for two or three days and juten (stuffed) tofu for four or five days.

You can also preserve tofu in various seasonings. It keeps for a long time, and you can enjoy unique flavors different from regular tofu. See pages 90-91 for methods of preserving tofu.

Preserved in soy sauce with garlic

Preserved in miso

Preserved in herb oil

Preserved in kochujang (hot bean mash)

CUTTING TECHNIQUES

Ingredients are cut in different ways, depending on the recipe, and tofu is no exception. Proper cutting allows seasonings to permeate them and also shortens the cooking time.

Cut in half vertically

Lay the tofu horizontally and cut in half vertically. Hold the tofu lightly with your left hand and draw the knife toward you.

Cut in half horizontally

Cut horizontally through the middle of the block of tofu. Hold it gently, so that it retains its form. This size is good for tofu "steak."

Cut into rectangular bars

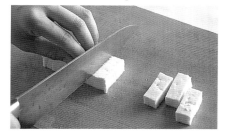

Lay the tofu on its side and cut it into bars of equal thickness.

Cut into quarters

Cut the tofu in half vertically and then horizontally. The quartered sizes are good for chilled tofu and deep-fried tofu.

Cut into thin slices

Lay the tofu sideways. Slice it from one end at equal intervals. The thickness of each slice should be 5 to 10 mm ($\frac{1}{8}$ to $\frac{1}{4}$ in).

Cut into cubes

Cut horizontally through the middle of the block of tofu and then dice the rectangle bars into cubes of equal size.

Cut into six parts

Cut horizontally through the middle of the block of tofu and then into three parts vertically. These cubes are good for stewed dishes.

Cut into square slices

Cut horizontally through the middle of the block of tofu. Cut the half into equal square slices from one end. This size is good for fried dishes.

Sooping

Scoop out the tofu with a spoon. This technique is usual ways of serving momen, silken, and basket tofu.

HOMEMADE FROZEN TOFU

Frozen tofu is easy to make and well worth trying. The homemade variety tastes a bit different than store bought variety, and its delicate flavor is suitable for any cuisine, either Japanese or Western.

INGREDIENTS

1 cake momen tofu

1 Drain the tofu in a bamboo colander and cut it into halves. Wrap each slab in plastic wrap.

3 The frozen state. The tofu takes on a yellowish tint.

5 When it thaws, the color returns to white, and the texture turns spongy.

2 Put the slabs in an airtight container or a freezer bag and freeze them.

4 Before using it, defrost it at room temperature or by heating it in a microwave oven for 4 to 5 minutes.

6 After defrosting, press the moisture out before using the tofu.
※Homemade frozen tofu should be used within 4 weeks.

SIMMERED FROZEN TOFU

Bacon gives a hearty taste to the frozen tofu, and peppercorns give it a bracing taste.

Ingredients

½ cake frozen tofu
2 slices bacon
4 stalks asparagus

Flavorings

1½ - 2 cups dashi stock
2 Tbsp light soy sauce
2 Tbsp sake
1 Tbsp mirin
½ tsp sugar
Dash of salt
1 tsp peppercorns

Method

❶Cut the bacon into 3 portions. Boil the asparagus and cut it into pieces, 5 cm (2 in) long.

❷Heat the frozen tofu in a microwave oven for 4 to 5 minutes to defrost it. Drain it well and cut into 8 triangles.

❸Combine the flavorings in a pot, add the bacon and tofu and cook. When the liquid comes to a boil, press down the solid ingredients with a small lid, and simmer over low heat for 7 to 8 minutes. Add the asparagus and cook for another 2 to 3 minutes.

SOUP AND ONE-POT DISHES

These standard recipes will bring a smile to your face. These recipes and variations were developed by professional chefs, and you can add them to your own repertoire.

SOUP

⚇VEGETABLE CHOWDER

The secret of its flavor is stir-frying the ingredients thoroughly in sesame oil.
Add this popular recipe to your repertoire.

O Ingredients

1 cake momen tofu
½ burdock root
½ carrot
140 g (5 oz) daikon radish
100 g (3½ oz) lotus root
1 scallion
1 tsp sesame oil
5 cups dashi stock
3 Tbsp soy sauce
2 Tbsp sake
⅓ tsp salt
Seven-spice pepper

O Method

❶Drain the tofu in a bamboo colander. Scrape the rind off the burdock root, rotating it to cut it into bite-sized random chunks and soak it in vinegared water. Cut the carrot and daikon radish into small pieces in the same way. Peel the lotus root and cut it into chunks. Soak the vegetables in water. Cut the scallion into pieces, 1 cm (⅜ in) long.
❷Heat the sesame and salad oil in a pot and stir-fry the burdock root, carrot, lotus root, and daikon radish in that order. Add the tofu, breaking it up as you continue stir-frying.
❸Add the dashi stock to the pot and bring it to a boil. Add the soy sauce, sake and salt. When it boils again, reduce the heat and simmer for 20 minutes.
❹Lastly, add the scallion and simmer for another 2 to 3 minutes. Sprinkle the mixture with seven-spice pepper, if desired.

VEGETABLE CHOWDER WITH MISO

This is a filling chowder with plenty of vegetables. Miso is used instead of soy sauce.

O Ingredients

1 cake momen tofu
140 g (5 oz) thin-sliced pork
4 taros
6 raw shiitake mushrooms
½ burdock root
80 g (2⅖ oz) carrot
1 scallion
½ block konnyaku
1½ Tbsp salad oil
6 cups dashi stock
4 Tbsp miso

O Method

❶Drain the tofu in a bamboo colander. Peel the taros, and rub them with salt to remove the slime. Cut them into quarters and then slice them crosswise. Shave the burdock root as if sharpening a pencil with a knife, and soak it in vinegared water. Shave the carrot in the same way. Trim the ends of the shiitake and cut them into four. Cut the scallion into round slices.

❷Cut the konnyaku into thin slabs and boil.

❸Heat the salad oil in a pot and stir-fry the chopped pork, burdock root, carrot, konnyaku, taros in that order. Add the tofu, breaking it up as you stir-fry. Pour in the dashi stock.

❹Bring the mixture to a boil and skim the scum as it rises. Add half of the miso and shiitake. When it boils again, reduce the heat, and simmer for about 10 minutes. Stir in the rest of the miso, and add the scallion. Simmer for another 1 to 2 minutes.

SICHUAN-STYLE HOT AND SOUR SOUP

This soup from China's Sichuan Province is characterized by a bracing yet refreshing flavor.

Ingredients
½ cake silken tofu
3 dried shiitake mushrooms
50 g (1¾ oz) bamboo shoots
50 g (1¾ oz) pork
1 tsp sake
Dash of salt
½ scallion
5 cups water
2 tsp instant chicken stock
Seasoning
  ⅔ tsp salt
  Dash pepper
  1 Tbsp each of sake and soy sauce
2 Tbsp vinegar
5 dissolved cornstarch (2 parts cornstarch and 3 parts water)
Coarsely ground black pepper

Method
❶Cut the tofu into sticks, 5 cm (2 in) long, 5 mm (⅛ in) wide and 5 mm (⅛ in) thick. Reconstitute the shiitake, trim off the hard stem tips, and cut into thin strips. Cut the bamboo shoots into thin strips. Cut the pork into pieces 5 mm (⅛ in) wide and season with sake and salt. Cut the scallion diagonally into thin slices.
❷Heat the water and instant chicken stock in a pot.
❸When the liquid came to a boil, add the pork, shiitake, and bamboo shoots, and simmer for 2 to 3 minutes. Add the seasonings, tofu, and scallion.
❹Thicken the broth by adding dissolved cornstarch. When it came to a boil, reduce the heat, add the vinegar, and turn off the heat.
❺Serve the soup in a bowl, sprinkling with coarsely ground black pepper.

EGG DROP SOUP WITH TOMATO AND TOFU

The egg in an egg soup must be light and fluffy. Children will enjoy this soup.

Ingredients
½ cake tofu (momen or silken)
1 egg
1 tomato
4 lettuce leaves
4 cups chicken stock
⅖ tsp salt
2 tsp sake
Dash of pepper

Method
❶Cut the tofu into rectangular bars.
❷Cut the tomato into bite-sized wedges. Cut the lettuce leaves into pieces 2 cm (¾ in) wide.
❸Heat the stock in a pot. When it comes to a boil, add the tomato pieces. Add the lettuce leaves and season with salt, sake, and pepper.
❹Beat the egg and swirl it gradually into the soup to make the pieces light and fluffy.

NAMEKO MUSHROOM SOUP

This unique soup of tofu and nameko mushrooms is accented with the crisp texture of celery.

O Ingredients

½ cake silken tofu
1 pack nameko mushrooms
½ stalk celery
5 cm (2 in) scallion
4 cups chicken stock
½ tsp salt
1 Tbsp sake

O Method

❶Cut the tofu into 1 cm (⅜ in) dices. Rinse the nameko mushrooms briefly in a colander. Remove the strings from the celery and cut it into julienne strips. Cut the scallion in the same way, soak it in water, and drain.
❷Heat the stock in a pot. When it comes to a boil, season with salt and sake. Add the nameko, tofu and celery. When the liquid boils again, skim the scum. Serve in a bowl topped with scallion.

CLEAR SOUP WITH DICED TOFU

Suitable for formal occasions. Beautifully diced tofu is one sign of a
Japanese cook's culinary skill.

Ingredients

1 cake momen tofu
3½ cups dashi stock (made from flakes of
dried bonito)
½ tsp salt
2 tsp soy sauce
1 Tbsp cornstarch
Dash of liquefied ginger
¼ sheet nori seaweed

Method

❶Cut the tofu into 5 mm (⅛ in) cumes.
❷Heat the dashi stock in a pot over
medium heat. When it comes to a boil,
season it with the salt and soy sauce and
add the tofu.
❸Dissolve the cornstarch in 1 tablespoon
of dashi stock, and add to the broth to
thicken.
❹Pour the soup into a bowl, and add a
dash of liquefied ginger. Top it with toasted
and crushed nori seaweed.

⁸SOYMILK SOUP WITH OYSTERS

Oysters in season go well with tofu. This is a dish with a Chinese-style flavor.

O Ingredients

½ cake silken tofu
150 g (5¼ oz) oysters
3½ cups chicken stock
(2 tsp instant soup stock)
⅔ cups soymilk
¾ tsp salt
Dash of pepper
1-2 Tbsp Chinese rice wine
5 cm (2 in) scallion, chopped
1 piece of fresh ginger, chopped
1 tsp salad oil

O Method

❶Rinse the oysters in salted water. Cut the tofu into rectangular pieces, 3 cm (1⅛ in) long, 1 cm (⅜ in) wide, and 1 cm (⅜ in) thick.

❷Heat the salad oil in a pot, and stir-fry the scallion and ginger. When you begin to smell them, add the stock. When the liquid comes to a boil, add the salt, pepper, Chinese rice wine, oysters, and tofu and simmer for 2 to 3 minutes.

❸Lastly, add the soymilk and bring the soup to a boil.

MOLOKHEIYA AND TOFU SOUP

A very nourishing soup flavored with aromatic vegetables and ground meat.

Ingredients

½ cake silken tofu
150 g (5¼ oz) molokheiya
60 g (2 oz) lean ground pork
1 tsp minced fresh ginger
10 cm (4 in) scallion, minced
½ Tbsp salad oil
3½ cups soup (made from 1 bouillon cube)
2 Tbsp sake
½ tsp salt
1 tsp soy sauce

Method

❶Cut the tofu into large chunks. Boil the molokheiya leaves briefly. Drain them and cut them into pieces, 2 cm (¾ in) long.

❷Heat the salad oil in a pot, and stir-fry the ginger and scallion over medium heat. When you can smell them, add the ground pork and stir-fry these ingredients together.

❸When the ground pork was separated, add the broth and sake, and bring the liquid to a boil. Skim the scum.

❹Add the molokheiya and simmer it over medium heat for 3 to 4 minutes. Add the tofu and season the soup with salt and soy sauce.

⚬ ONE-POT DISH WITH KIMCHI

A popular Korean favorite. It is enjoyable to decide what you add at the end of the meal.

⚬ Ingredients

1 cake grilled tofu
250 g (9 oz) kimchi (Korean spicy pickled vegetables)
200 g (7 oz) end pieces of beef
1 pack Chinese chives
1 scallion
150 g (5¼ oz) bean sprouts
1 piece of fresh ginger, minced
1 clove garlic, minced
10 cm (4 in) scallion, minced
1-2 Tbsp sesame oil

Broth

5 cups chicken stock
1½ Tbsp miso
1-2 Tbsp soy sauce
2 tsp kochujang (see p. 91)

⚬ Method

❶ Squeeze the liquid from the kimchi and set it aside. Cut it into uneven strips, 5 cm (2 in) long. Cut the tofu into cubes, 1 cm (⅜ in) thick. Cut the Chinese chives into pieces, 5 cm (2 in) long. Cut the scallion diagonally into thick slices. Remove the roots from the bean sprouts.

❷ Heat the sesame oil in a pot, and stir-fry the minced scallion, garlic and ginger over low heat. When you can smell the mixture, add the kimchi, and stir-fry. Mix in the combined broth ingredients, and bring to a boil briefly.

❸ When the liquid comes to a boil, add the beef, Chinese chives, scallion, bean sprouts, and tofu. Eat it while it is still hot. You may adjust the flavor by pouring in liquid from the kimchi, to taste.

※ You may add cooked rice, noodles or mochi. Some ingredients are not suitable for an earthenware pot, so take care.

⁛SIMMERED TOFU WITH MISO

An distinctive simmered tofu dish that has a slightly sweet taste.

O Ingredients

1 cake momen tofu
1 small burdock root
1 small carrot
2 dried shiitake mushrooms
5 cups dashi stock
80 - 100 g (2⅘ - 3½ oz) red miso
2½ - 3 Tbsp sugar

O Method

❶Cut the tofu into 8 cubes. Shave the burdock root as if sharpening a pencil with a knife, and soak it in vinegared water. Shave the carrot in the same way. Trim the hard ends of shiitake mushrooms and cut them in half.
❷Heat the dashi stock in a pot and bring it to a boil. Dissolve the miso in it and add sugar.
❸Add the tofu, burdock root, and carrot to the pan, and simmer over low heat, taking care not to let the mixture boil, until the ingredients are cooked through.

⊗ONE-DISH POT WITH TOFU DUMPLINGS

You will love these fluffy soft tofu dumplings floating in a delicious broth.

○ Ingredients
1 cake momen tofu
200 g (7 oz) ground chicken
Flavorings
 2 Tbsp minced scallion
 1 tsp liquefied ginger
 1 Tbsp sake
 ⅖ tsp salt
 1 egg, beaten
 6 Tbsp cornstarch
30 g (1 oz) Japanese trefoil
2 packs shimeji mushrooms
6 cups dashi stock
1 tsp each of salt and soy sauce

○ Method
❶Drain the tofu completely, and wrap it in a paper towel to get rid of the extra moisture.
❷Add the tofu and the flavorings to the ground chicken, and mix them into a paste with a mortar and pestle or in a food processor.
❸Cut the trefoil into pieces, 5 cm (2 in) long. Trim the hard ends of the shimeji mushrooms and separate it.
❹Heat the dashi stock in a pot, and bring it to a boil. Scoop up the tofu-chicken mixture with a spoon and drop into the stock. Season with salt and soy sauce. Simmer over low heat 1 to 2 minutes. Add the shimeji mushrooms and simmer for another 2 to 3 minutes. Lastly, top it with Japanese trefoil.

⊗SOYMILK SOUP

A white soup using soymilk as a base. It goes well with smooth silken tofu.

○ Ingredients
1 cake silken tofu
1 pack shimeji mushrooms
1 pack enoki mushrooms
1 bundle potherb mustard
½ bundle chives
4 cups soymilk
Broth
 2 cups dashi stock
 2 tsp soy sauce
 ½ tsp salt

○ Method
❶Cut the tofu into 6 cubes. Trim off the hard ends of the shimeji and enoki mushrooms, and separate them. Cut the potherb mustard and chives into pieces, 5 cm (2 in) long, and separate them.
❷Heat the soymilk in a pot over medium heat. When it ccmes to a boil, lower the flame. Mix in the broth ingredients and when the liquid boils again, reduce the heat to medium. Add the solid ingredients and serve piping hot.
※Soymilk scorches easily, so lower the flame while the ingredients are cooking.

HOME MADE YUBA

If thick soymilk is gently heated, a thin film covers its surface. This film is called yuba. Homemade yuba is a true delicacy. You can eat it each newly formed layer until the soymilk in the pot is exhausted. You can hardly wait to see the film form.

Ingredients

1 bottle soymilk
Wasabi (Japanese horseradish)
Soy sauce

Method

Heat the soymilk in a pot over medium heat. Lower the flame just before it comes to a boil. When a thin film is formed, transfer it to a bowl with chopsticks, and eat it with some soy sauce and wasabi.

DESSERTS

Tofu desserts of tofu are low in calories, and you can eat as much as you like. Enjoy its natural flavor.

⚇ HONG KONG-STYLE TOFU DESSERT

This dessert is popular in Hong Kong. Eat it warm with sesame seeds and soybean flour.

O Ingredients
1 cake silken tofu
4 Tbsp honey
4 Tbsp hot water
Ground sesame seeds
Soybean flour

O Method
❶Dissolve the honey in hot water and mix well.
❷Put the tofu in a heatproof container and cover with plastic wrap. Heat for 2 minutes, and transfer to a bowl.
❸Pour the honey over the tofu, and sprinkle it with sesame seeds and soybean flour.

⦂COCONUT ICE

Tofu makes the coconut flavor less intense.
The delicate texture is like sherbet.

O **Ingredients**
1 cake silken tofu
100 g (3½ oz) sugar
¾ cup coconut milk

O **Method**
❶Blend the tofu, sugar and coconut
milk together in a blender until smooth
and creamy.
❷Pour the mixture into a metal
container and cover with plastic wrap.
❸Freeze the mixture in a freezer
overnight. Beat it two or three times
during the freezing process to make the
texture more airy.

JELLIED TOFU TOPPED WITH SWEETENED BEANS

When the jelly began to set, top it with add sweetened beans for an attractive presentation.

Ingredients

1 cake silken tofu
4 g (⅛ oz) powdered agar
1 cup water
50 g (1¾ oz) sugar
20-30 g (⅔-1 oz) sweetened ama natto beans

Method

❶Drain the tofu in a bamboo colander. Blend it into a paste-like consistency.

❷Put the powdered agar and water in a pot and let stand for 5 minutes.

❸Heat the agar mixture until it comes to a boil. Add the sugar and mix well. When everything is dissolved, remove from the heat.

❹Mix the tofu and agar mixture well and pour into a mold. Top it with sweetened beans and chill in the refrigerator until set.

⦂TOFU AND RICE-FLOUR DUMPLINGS

Adzuki beans, molasses and soybean flour

Tofu-flavored Japanese-style sweets. Fans of rice flour dumplings will be in heaven.

○ **Ingredients**
¼ cake momen tofu
1 cup rice flour
½ cup water
Boiled adzuki beans
Molasses
Soybean flour

○ **Method**
❶Crumble the tofu into the rice flour and knead well. Add water little by little, and continue kneading until the dough becomes stiff.
❷Roll the dough into 1- 1.5 cm (⅜ - ½ in) balls, press the center with your finger, and shape them into disks.
❸Drop the dough disks in boiling water. When they float to the surface, scoop them into cold water and drain.
❹Transfer the dumplings to a bowl and eat them with adzuki beans, molasses and soybean flour.

JELLIED TOFU WITH HONEY AND LEMON JUICE

Subtle flavors of honey and lemon gradually increase in intensity. Mash the tofu well to make it smooth.

O **Ingredients**

½ cake silken tofu
5 g (⅙ oz) powdered gelatin
50 g (1¾ oz) honey
1½ Tbsp lemon juice
Water

O **Method**

❶Soak the powdered gelatin in 3 tablespoons of water. Wrap the tofu in a paper towel and drain it in a bamboo colander.

❷Mash the tofu and beat with an egg beater until smooth. Add the honey and lemon juice.

❸Bring ⅓ cup of water to a boil and turn off the heat. Dissolve the gelatin in it, add the tofu, and mix well. Pour the mixture into a mold and let it chill in the refrigerator until set.

:SOUFFLÉ-STYLE TOFU

Healthful, with a warm cake-like texture.
Bake it like a soft, light soufflé.

○ **Ingredients (4 servings)**
200 g (7 oz) momen tofu
120 g (4⅕ oz) honey
3 egg yolks
30 g (1 oz) cake flour
1 tsp grated lemon peel
Juice of 1 lemon
½ Tbsp rum
1½ egg whites

○ **Method**
❶Drain the tofu in a bamboo colander, and wrap it in a paper towel to drain off any extra moisture.
❷Beat the tofu with a beater until smooth. Add 80 g (2⅘ oz) of honey and mix well. Add the egg yolks and mix together thoroughly.
❸Add the sifted cake flour, lemon peel, lemon juice, and rum, and mix thoroughly.
❹Beat the egg whites. Mix in the honey, dividing it into two portions, first 20 g (⅔ oz) and then the rest, and mix. Beat together until frothy.
❺Divide the honey-egg white mixture into two portions. Add the first half to the batter and mix, and then add and mix the rest.
❻Pour ❺ into cocottes and bake on the lower rack of an oven preheated to 160℃ -170℃ （320° F- 340° F） for 40 to 50 minutes.

⦂SOYMILK PUDDING

This homemade custard has a natural sweetness.

○ Ingredients (for 3 - 4 puddings)
1⅓ cups soymilk
50 g (1¾ oz) sugar
2 Tbsp water
1 tsp water
2 large eggs
40 g (1⅖ oz) honey
1 Tbsp rum
Dash of vanilla extract

○ Method
❶Heat the sugar and 2 tablespoons of water in a small pot over low heat. When the mixture turns brown, add 1 teaspoon of water to make caramel sauce.
❷Butter pudding moulds, and pour equal portions of the caramel sauce into each one.
❸Heat the soymilk in a pot and mix in the honey. Let it cool.
❹Beat the eggs, add the soymilk mixture, and strain. Mix in the rum and vanilla extract.
❺Pour the mixture into the moulds until each is 80% full.
❻Cover a baking tray with hot water, and place the moulds in them. Bake them in an oven preheated to 180℃ (360˚ F) for 20 to 25 minutes. Insert a skewer to test for doneness. Let them cool slightly and then chill them in the refrigerator.

ITALIAN MOUSSE

Nothing could be simpler: just mix the ingredients. If the fruit is frozen, you will end up with a gelato-like dessert.

Ingredients
½ cake silken tofu
60 g (2 oz) raspberries
40 g (1⅖ oz) sugar
Some raspberries for decoration

Method
❶Wrap the tofu in a paper towel, put it in a bamboo colander and chill it in the refrigerator. Chill the raspberries in the refrigerator, too.
❷Blend the tofu, berries and sugar together in a blender.
❸Serve the mixture in a bowl topped with raspberries.

About the auther Junko Takagi

Junko Takagi is devoted to a new type of cooking that suits modern lifestyles and satisfies everyone's tastes. The ingredients she uses for her new cuisine are all readily available. She never uses chemical seasonings, and makes the best use of the ingredients. "Healthful Cooking of Fruit and Vegetables," the fruit of her study of dietetics is highly rated by many people in various fields. She also teaches people how to make use of electric appliances such as microwave ovens and suggests new ideas for improving our dietary habits. Her engaging personality and her unique way of speaking have endeared her to audiences everywhere.